YOU MET HER
WHERE?!

Courtney,

Thank you so much for being a guest with us on our podcast/radio show. You were FANTASTIC!. Not sure if you are much of a reader, but here is our story. Pray it will be a blessing to you in some way.

Kevin & Stephanie

Mark 11:24

YOU MET HER WHERE?!

WHERE?!

Our Journey of Healing, Hope and Hot Wings

Kevin + Stephanie Mason

TO

Emme, Elle, and Tate.
You were our inspiration for writing this book.
May this serve as a reminder to you and future
generations of what God has done.

TABLE OF CONTENTS

INTRODUCTION

Why Am I Writing This Book?

This is the question I keep asking myself. I hate writing. I mean I *really* do not like to write. I get a little nauseous and sick to my stomach just thinking about writing a book. I asked my wife, Stephanie, last night if she thought I should just write a long article instead. She laughed out loud and then never gave me an answer. She knows how long I have been talking about the idea of this book, praying about this book, and then of course, procrastinating writing this book.

My intent is to write a book that will help others who may be facing a hopeless situation. When I was going through cancer treatments at The James Cancer Hospital in Columbus, Ohio, I was so appreciative with how helpful all the nurses, doctors, and surgeons had been to me. I wondered if there was something I could do to make an impact for others like these incredible people had done for me. My initial idea was to attempt a career change by exploring a move into healthcare finance. I realized I would only be helping others indirectly, but it would personally be more meaningful to me.

As of the time I am writing this, I have eighteen years of accounting and finance experience in Big 4 public accounting and with a couple of Fortune 500 companies. I have been blessed to have worked for some great companies in my career including Limited Brands (now L Brands),

JPMorgan Chase, and Express. I hoped there might be an opportunity for me to use my professional experience behind the scenes in health care to help others. Unfortunately at my level, I found out that hospitals are not willing to hire someone without a minimum of five years experience in health care. Even though I have my CPA (certified public accountant) license and MBA (master of business administration) degree, not having that industry experience was apparently a deal breaker for the hospitals and healthcare companies I met with.

However, in my pursuit of wanting to help others, things kept pointing me toward writing a book.

"You know what you should do…"

Over the past year, we have had multiple friends, family, coworkers, or acquaintances randomly tell us that we should write a book. The conversation will typically start out with "You know what you should do…" I love it when people volunteer their unsolicited opinion to me (that was sarcasm).

I know this may sound harsh, but I will thank people for their free spirited advice and then completely ignore whatever they told me. I understand most people have good intentions, but to be honest here, I am not going to take book advice from someone who doesn't even read books! That's like me telling our family doctor, "Hey doc, you know what you should do? Go cure cancer. You could make a boatload of money if you did that!"

I typically will only consider personal opinions from just a handful of people I trust and am close with. However, after hearing *multiple* people tell us, "You know what you should do," I started to think there might be something to this. I realize Stephanie and I have some crazy stories to share after having gone through some pretty traumatic, life-threatening events. But do I *really* feel like writing a book about it?

Answer: nope.

~~Strikethrough~~

As an FYI...whenever you see a word or phrase in this book that ~~looks like this,~~ you can assume the crossed out word(s) are what I (Kevin) *actually* meant or was thinking. In most cases, Steph has asked me to delete or replace these word(s) with something a little more warm and kindhearted. And in most cases, I have decided to just cross out my original word(s) for your entertainment.

> To illustrate, here is an excerpt from Chapter 1...
> *"If you have ever met my wife, you will immediately notice her bubbly disposition and compassion for people ~~NOT named Kevin Mason.~~"*

God, Can You Give Me a Sign?

I have been trying to rationalize why I should spend hours...upon hours...upon hours of my very limited free time to write a book about our personal lives. I just cringe thinking about the colossal effort required to write a book. I mean, who really wants to hear what I have to say... about me? Would anyone even read it? I have no idea, but I do know there were a few signs that proved I should write *something*.

Sign #1

The initial idea of a book actually came from someone I worked with. While going through cancer treatments, I had a lot of people contact me to tell me they were thinking of me or praying for me. To keep them informed of how my surgery and subsequent treatments were going, I decided to email everyone a few health updates. At the end of each email, I would share a funny story about something that had happened to me.

After sending out a couple of emails, I was blown away by the reactions from friends, family, and coworkers. A lot of the responses were typically people thanking me for making *their* day! I was shocked to read that some folks had been reading my emails *multiple* times. Some had even forwarded them to their family and friends to read, while others told me how they thought my stories were hilarious.

But there was one response that stood out among them all. One of the marketing directors I worked with shared with me how her father had recently been diagnosed with cancer. He was in his seventies and had not been given a favorable outlook. She had been reading him my emails and doing her best to encourage him by what I had been sharing about my treatments. After one of my emails, she responded with, "Kevin, you need to somehow publish these."

Sign #2

This past fall, I started seriously praying about the idea of writing a book. I didn't know if this might be something God was leading me to do or if this might be one gigantic waste of time. During the same week I started praying about this book idea, I went on a white water rafting trip with a friend of mine. When I met him at his house for the trip, his wife introduced me to someone I had never met before. In the process of introducing me, she mentioned how Stephanie and I had an amazing testimony to share and could even write a book about it. It was a random statement Michelle had made, and she may not even remember saying it. However, it got my attention. This felt like some type of a "sign" that I needed to write a ~~children's~~ book.

Sign #3

At one of my previous employers, we had a quarterly meeting called a "Gratitude Gathering," where the entire home office of about 800 associates would gather in the foyer to listen to some encouraging, motivational comments from the CEO. At the end of his brief comments that were typically NOT motivating at all, the CEO would read a handful of grat-itude / thank you cards that associates had written to someone else in the company. If your card was read, you and the person written to would receive a gift card to Amazon or Starbucks. Since these meetings had commenced about two years earlier, I had never taken the time to write a note to someone (although I should have). However, I noticed in prior meetings the cards "randomly" selected were typically over-the-top nice or slightly humorous. I honestly think HR just glanced through the cards ahead of time and handpicked a few ~~that might keep associates awake after the non-motivational speech.~~

Before one particular meeting, I decided to write a thank you note to one of my direct reports to: first, tell him how great of a job he was doing; second, try to win him something that I wouldn't have to pay for; and third, test my writing skills. I was curious to see if my note might be good enough to be "randomly" selected.

Well, if this was a test, by the grace of God, I aced it! Not only was my thank you card selected, but the CEO had a tough time reading it. It was not because couldn't read my handwriting or because he strug-gles with reading. (Sound it out!) He had a hard time reading my note because he started laughing. Then the entire home office started laughing. I remember the person standing next to me saying, "You are really funny, Kevin Mason!" I then had to walk up front with Eric to receive our gift cards. On the way back to my standing-room-only spot, colleagues were applauding and some even gave me a high five. I had all of a sudden turned into Mr. Popular at work, which was a new experience for me.

While On the Subject: If you have ever seen the movie *Four Christmases*, I kind of felt like Vince Vaughn's character when he played Joseph in the church Christmas play. In that movie, he comically gets a newfound burst of confidence when he receives a standing ovation for his performance in the play. He starts dramatically high-fiving church members while walking back to his seat. I laugh out loud HARD every time I watch that scene.

Later that afternoon, while still reeling from my "Joseph moment," I had a colleague go out of her way to find me at my desk. She wanted to thank me for making her laugh. She mentioned she had been having a rough day and needed to laugh that afternoon. That had never…I mean, *never* EVER happened to me before. To me, this was another sign ~~that I needed to make a photo book~~.

Do It for the Kids

After reminding myself of these three separate experiences, I am finally convinced that I should probably write a book. If nobody actually reads this book, it will not be a complete waste of time. The reason: Emme, Elle, and Tate.

I want to document our story for these three kids. As you will read, all three of our children have been absolute miracles. I want them to know how much we wanted them, how much we prayed for them, and what it took for us to have each one of them. It took a lot of faith. It took some *crazy* faith! Hopefully, this book will teach them how to trust God through life's storms and let them know how much they are loved.

Time to Turn Our Lives into an Open Book

Listen, I am a very private guy. I actually do not like talking about myself and typically try to talk about any other topic. However, I realize our privacy is about to end. Stephanie and I have a very unique story to share. I mean…the *multiple* things God has brought us through are so unusual it's almost NOT believable. Being the professional skeptic that I am, I might not believe some of these stories if I hadn't actually lived them—from my wife getting electrocuted, having a brain tumor, struggling to conceive a baby, being devastated by a miscarriage, to my cancer diagnosis at the age of thirty-seven.

As a man of faith, I feel this book is somehow part of my assignment to help others grow closer to God. I believe God is wanting turn our lives into an open book to give some hope to others. As you will read, we have lived through some devastating life events and, by the grace of God, survived to write about them.

This is our journey.

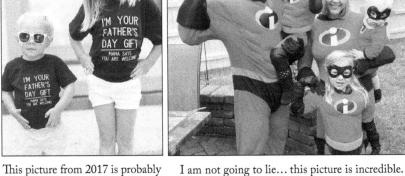

This picture from 2017 is probably   I am not going to lie… this picture is incredible.
my favorite Father's Day gift.

CHAPTER 1

HOW WE MET

Kevin and Stephanie

As I begin to write this book, my goal is to be brutally honest with you. I am not writing this in an attempt to make Stephanie or myself look good or appear to be something we are not. I am writing this to try to help those of you who may be facing your own Goliaths in life (i.e., a giant, colossal mountain of a problem that only God can help you with). By the end of this book, we want everyone to know the power of God is real. Through our stories, we will share what we have learned about healing through each step of our journey.

To do that, we will have to be genuine and authentic with you. I am not interested in presenting some type of fictional or fabricated view of our lives. You see enough of that on Facebook and Instagram.

This means you are going to read about the amazing things God has brought us through. We have faced more than our fair share of Goliaths over the past fifteen years. You will also read about some of the dumb stuff I have done. Notice I used the word "I" instead of "we" in that last sentence. That's because my wife doesn't do dumb stuff. Apparently, I do enough of that for the both of us. More than once, my wife has given me her confused look that says, "How can you be so smart at some things... and then so stupid at others?"

I don't know. I guess it's a gift!

Before we jump into the heavy stuff we have faced, like cancer and electrocution, I should introduce ourselves and give you a little bit of our background. That may help give you some context when you read our stories. For those of you who do not know us, you are about to. For those of you who do know us, your name will probably pop up somewhere in this book. (Sorry. I probably should have cleared that with you first.)

If you do happen to know us personally, I think it's safe to say you will probably be surprised at some point by what you will read. Unless you are part of our immediate family, there will *definitely* be a few things you were not aware of.

Kevin's Perspective: Who Is Stephanie Mason?

I have now been married to Stephanie Mason for fifteen years. Let me tell you about her.

In the most complimentary way possible, I would describe my wife as a unicorn. She is intelligent, athletic, a sports fan, has an incredible personality, AND happens to be gorgeous! She is also a wonderful mother to our three children and a compassionate nurse to anyone NOT named Kevin Mason (more on that later). Like a unicorn, she is someone I was told did not exist. I'll explain.

Almost two decades ago when I was single, I made a wish list of about thirty qualities I was looking for in a future spouse. This was me dreaming about what I thought the perfect woman looked like. Most of the items on my list were pretty darn crazy and completely unrealistic. Quite honestly, I didn't even meet the criteria myself. For some dumb reason, I thought my future soul mate should or would meet these colossal standards.

In hindsight, there were a few items NOT on my list that I wish I would have included. For example, nowhere on my list did I mention my future spouse should be a multimillionaire. (Stephanie, that was a joke!)

My list was thrown away a long time ago, but I do remember several of the items. In no particular order, the perfect wife for me would be:

❖ Gorgeous
❖ Athletic (I would love to be able to play sports with her, like tennis or golf.)
❖ Smart (would have a college degree).
❖ Professional job with favorable work hours (possibly a teacher, since they get all weekends, holidays, snow days, and summers off).
❖ Christian (have a personal relationship with God).
❖ Pure (saving herself for marriage).
❖ From a great family (preferably a close-knit family that did not believe in divorce).
❖ Gorgeous (Apparently I was looking for a trophy wife.)
❖ Sports fan (I loved all sports, especially watching college football. Living in Columbus, I would love it if she would enjoy watching Ohio State football with me.)
❖ Funny (have a great personality and be able to laugh together).
❖ Content with staying home at times (I did not like to go out much back then because it made me uncomfortable. Before I met Stephanie, I was a little insecure, a little awkward with some social anxiety.)
❖ Want to have children
❖ Socially savvy (Able to adapt to any environment—i.e., around my friends, other women, church folks, professional work parties, ~~cray cray~~ relatives—she would need to be a chameleon!)
❖ Authentic (Someone I could be myself around. I could be silly with her and not feel embarrassed. I could let my guard down and just be me. Someone who would like the real, unedited, behind the scenes version of me.)

- ❖ Affectionate (She would make me feel loved.)
- ❖ Gorgeous (Did I mention she would be a blonde bombshell?)

This might only be about half of the list I had written down, but you get my point. Very unrealistic. Very unfair expectations. I was looking for a unicorn.

Not the Answer I Was Expecting

I showed my list to only one person. That person was Micah, who was one of my closest friends (still is) and someone I could completely trust (still can). Micah grew up as a pastor's kid (like I did), was five years older than me, married, and had recently become a father. I felt he would be a great person to speak with about dating.

This sounds absolutely terrible, but I think I let him read my list so he could be on the lookout for any young, single ladies who might fit my criteria. To show you how naive I was, I actually thought Micah was going to read my list and say something along the lines of, "Oh yeah, I know of at least three or four single women off the top of my head my wife and I could set you up with. There is Rebecca in Charlotte we met a few months ago…and then Elizabeth from Nashville, who is the definition of a Southern belle. Man, I wish you would have showed me your list sooner!"

However, when he read my list, he literally just started laughing. Out loud. Kind of hard. It turned into a "you are starting to hurt my feelings" kind of laugh.

In the middle of his laughter, I remember him saying, "AND SHE HAS TO HAVE A COLLEGE DEGREE?!"

Followed by more laughing.

After his laughter finally subsided and he caught his breath, he told me he was going to have to be brutally honest with me. To my disappointment, Micah told me he didn't know any girls even close to meeting my outrageous list. He said, "Kevin, I have literally been to hundreds of churches across North America as a teenager, a student in Bible college, and a traveling evangelist. I hate to tell you this, but I am not sure the type of girl you are looking for even exists."

NOT the answer I was expecting.

Crazy, Good News

You want to hear some good news? Like some crazy, good news? A year later, I found my unicorn.

Her name was Stephanie Keller.

> *Disclaimer:* This unicorn did not actually meet all thirty of the criteria from my list of ridiculousness. However, since she did check off twenty-seven of the thirty boxes, I went ahead and made an exception.

I soon found out Stephanie was the type of kid growing up I wish I could have been. In high school, she had a 3.95 GPA, was a member of the National Honor Society, played three sports (cross-country, basketball, softball), was homecoming attendant multiple times, blah, blah, blah.

She was an All-State softball player in high school and part of two state tournament teams, before playing in college at Mt. Vernon Nazarene, an NAIA school in Ohio. After playing three seasons at "The Naz," Stephanie transferred to Capital University to finish her nursing degree. Then after college, she passed her nursing exam to become a registered nurse and worked at two different hospitals in cardiac, labor and delivery, and neurosurgery. She now works part-time at a medical spa and absolutely loves her job. On top of that, Stephanie is an amazing mother, wife, and puts up with me on a daily basis.

If you have ever met my wife, you will immediately notice her bubbly personality and compassion for people NOT named Kevin Mason.

> ***Warning*:** Stephanie is a big-time hugger. Be prepared because she will give you a big hug around your neck, whether you like hugs or not. She doesn't care. Stephanie about crushed my very introverted eighty-year-old Uncle David one year at Thanksgiving. He went to politely shake my wife's hand and ended up getting probably the biggest bear hug of his life. That hug put the biggest smile on his face and made my entire family bust out laughing. We hadn't seen Uncle David smile like that in years! Like others in my family (who shall remain nameless), I think he now likes Stephanie more than me.

After fifteen years of marriage, I am used to this treatment by now. If you have ever met us, you are more likely to remember my wife than me. You might remember her name but probably not mine. You may even refer to me as "Stephanie's husband," like some folks do at our church. I am totally fine with that…because my wife is pretty amazing. She is like a unicorn!

Not-So-Good News

After marrying a unicorn, I soon learned they can be a little tricky to live with at times. Apparently, you have to constantly feed them. Unicorns can get a little cranky and will even snap at you when they are hungry OR pregnant. And when they are both, you should try to work late.

Steph, I am kidding! (But not really.)

Who Is Kevin Mason?
(written by Stephanie Mason)

I guess it is my turn to tell you about my husband. Let me start by saying how much I love Kevin. But if you only knew how naive he was when we first met! Oh my goodness!

He was the most sheltered, innocent guy I had ever met. Now to be fair to him, Kevin was raised in a very strict Christian home with a minister for a father. He was a pastor's kid his entire childhood and I am sure needed to be a good boy at all times, especially in front of church people. Even though I grew up in the Lutheran church with my family, his upbringing was *vastly* different from mine.

However, when I first met Kevin, I definitely got butterflies in my stomach. I remember seeing him in a red T-shirt and jeans with his hat on backwards, thinking, *This guy is really cute!* I was just praying he was not another dumb jock like I had met in the past. Thank God, he actually turned out to be one of the smartest and most intelligent guys I had ever met.

Like Kevin, I, too, had a list of qualities I wanted in a future spouse. It wasn't nearly as long or specific as his list, nor did I write them down. But here is what I remember:

❖ I wanted him to be a Christian.
❖ I wanted him to be athletic. I love to work out and wanted a future spouse to enjoy working out as well.
❖ I wanted him to be in the medical field or a business guy. I thought both professions would make good money for a family. Plus, I thought it would be cute to see my husband in scrubs or carrying a briefcase.
❖ I wanted him to come from a good family that would accept me as their own.
❖ I wanted him to love sports as much as I did.
❖ I wanted him to be personally driven and not settle for mediocrity.
❖ I wanted to be able to laugh with him.
❖ Finally, I wanted to find him attractive and get butterflies when I was around him.

Surprisingly, Kevin checked off almost everything on my list.

———————————————————

Kevin's Response

What in the world is my wife talking about? I was expecting to read how I ADDED things to her list!

The Story of How We Met

As you will see, we have a lot of unique and sometimes amusing stories to share, including the story of how we met. I would guess there are only a few people who know (or actually remember) the entire story. It's not that we are embarrassed or trying to hide something from our past. However, unless I know you pretty well, I will not go out of my way to share all the details with you.

Typically, if someone asks me how Stephanie and I met, I will tell them my dad introduced us (which is true). If they continue with a follow-up question like, "Where did your dad meet Stephanie?" I will answer with, "He met her at some restaurant she worked at in college" (also true). If that person continues to dig with *another* follow-up question like, "What restaurant did she work at?" I may tell them, "Denny's" (which is NOT true). I have given out the "Denny's" answer multiple times, including when my mom met Stephanie for the first time. Then I have to follow it up with mentioning how much I love the Grand Slam meal at Denny's (also NOT true).

I actually did this recently with our six-year-old daughter, Emme. She is so smart (like her mother) and so freaking inquisitive. She kept drilling me with questions, but I really didn't want to have this conversation with her just yet. She probably asked more follow-up questions than any adult has in the past. This could be due to adults typically being able to read my nonverbal cues that say, "Stop grilling me with questions!"

Since kindergarteners are not good at reading anything, I had to face a lengthy cross-examination from Emme. After each answer I gave, I would see her try to process it in her mind to see if it made sense to her... and then ask me another question. I was actually really impressed by her line of questioning. But gosh, I hope she doesn't turn into an attorney someday. I don't want our future family dinners ending with me yelling, "JUST EAT YOUR FOOD! NO MORE QUESTIONS!"

Well, Emme, here is the truth. I hope you can handle it.

Also, I am sorry for ~~lying~~ misleading you when you were six years old.

Thank You, Dad!

When I met Stephanie in July 2002, I was twenty-three years old, a social amateur, very conservative, and very naive about girls and life. I was focused on my new accounting career, studying for the CPA exam, and playing on a travel slow-pitch softball team (2003 Ohio Class D State Champions). Like most weekends back then, I was playing in a softball tournament over the Fourth of July weekend. Unlike most weekends, though, my dad called to see if I was playing somewhere locally so he could come watch. On that Saturday, my dad and his new wife of only a few months showed up and watched me play in the first two games of the tournament.

About two hours after they had left, I got a phone call from my dad while I was waiting for our next game to start. The conversation went something like this:

Me: "Hey Dad, what's up?"

Dad: "You are NOT going to believe this!"

Me: "Believe what?"

Dad: "Kevin, we just met the PERFECT girl for you!"
       (I was VERY skeptical, especially since my dad had tried to play this love connection game with me before.)

Me: "Uh...I doubt it. Where did you meet her?"

Dad: "HOOTERS!"

Me: "You met her *WHERE?!*"

Dad: "HOOTERS!

Me: "Dad, what are you doing at Hooters?"

Dad: "Oh my gosh, Kevin…that place has THE BEST key lime pie!"

Me: "Yeah…sure they do."

After they had left the tournament, my dad and his new wife wanted to get lunch somewhere before heading home. Apparently, they had eaten some key lime pie on their recent honeymoon in Key West, Florida. While driving, they saw a billboard for Hooters that mentioned having key lime pie. That sign reminded them of their honeymoon and now they were craving some pie. Knowing my dad, I actually believed him when he told me he went to Hooters "for the key lime pie" (especially since he went there with his wife). However, if anyone else on earth would have told me this same story, I would have immediately called BS.

Any whoooo…my dad told me they had met some blonde bombshell named Stephanie, who had been their waitress. After they ~~harassed~~ questioned Stephanie about her personal life, they told her she *had* to meet Ron's son (me). What they didn't know was Stephanie had just broken things off earlier that week with some ~~clown / hobo / hilljack~~ other guy. She had literally only been single for a few hours!

This was some impeccable timing. Thankfully, my dad asked Stephanie when she would be working the following weekend ~~because he is creepy like that~~. She told him Friday night, not thinking he was actually serious. Well, he was very serious. My dad was apparently trying to handpick his future daughter-in-law.

He Was Not Asking Me

That following week, my dad was persistent that I go to Hooters with him. He was not asking me. He was telling me. I told him I was busy. He didn't believe me. I told him I would be studying for the CPA exam that Friday night because I had a softball tournament on Saturday and Sunday. He would not take no for an answer. He told me to study a little bit after work and then he would pick me up around 8:00 p.m. He was adamant that I meet this girl.

After realizing I wasn't going to win this argument, I reluctantly agreed. I thought it would be a good opportunity for me to spend some time with my dad AND a good opportunity for me to get a free meal.

"That's Fine. You Can Sit in the Car."

The next Friday night, my dad picked me up at my apartment. As soon as I got in the car, I felt uncomfortable (shocker). After driving about ten minutes, we got to the exit ramp for Route 161, and I told my dad to turn around. I didn't want to go. For one, it felt really weird having my dad play wingman by introducing me to some random girl he had just met. And two, I did not want my first experience at Hooters to be with my dad.

That sounds really funny now, but it is the honest truth. My dad kept driving and said, "That's fine. You can sit in the car. I am going to go eat some wings and say hello to Stephanie."

Then we had awkward silence for the remainder of the car ride. There was no radio on or talking until we got to the restaurant. I was mad and incredibly uncomfortable. Like usual, my dad was NOT going to listen to me. His mind was already made up. He wanted to go eat some chicken wings (and probably some key lime pie). After he parked the car, I was still mad and didn't move from the passenger seat. My dad turned off the car, got out, and started walking toward the restaurant. At this point, I was thinking about my current predicament. If I just stayed in the car:

1. I was going to get bored real quick (the iPhone had not been invented yet).
2. I was going to get hot real quick (it was July).
3. I guarantee you, I would get made fun of by my dad in front of this girl. I could see my dad saying something like, "Hey Steph, would you mind taking these extra wings out to my son? Just look for a blue Toyota Corolla with a twenty-three-year-old sitting in the passenger seat by himself."

My dad would absolutely do #3, and that potential embarrassment would be worse than me just saying hello to some random girl at Hooters. (I recently had my dad read this story to confirm the accuracy of my details. He laughed and then agreed he would have done something like #3 if I had not gotten out of the car.)

By the time my dad got to the sidewalk, I decided to get out of the car. Not a big deal. I would just briefly meet this girl and then eat some free wings. Heck, I might even order some wings to go just to get back at my dad for this awkward situation.

After we got inside, we had to wait a few minutes to be able to sit at one of Stephanie's tables. I remember looking around the restaurant. Is that Stephanie? Nope. Is that Stephanie? God, I hope not! How about that one?

After we finally sat down at one of her tables, a waitress came over to say hello. She was really cute, really energetic, really over-the-top smiling, and super happy. This was not my future wife. However, this was my future sister-in-law, Katie Keller (now Katie Schnetzer). She had come over to say hello and let us know her sister was finishing something up in the back (i.e., sprinting to the bathroom to freshen up).

Little did I know Katie was actually coming over to kill time and give me the initial screening. My theory is that my dad gave off the vibe he was a creeper, and Katie wanted to ensure his son was somewhat normal. (My dad does not agree with this theory.) Thankfully, I passed the initial interview screening, and after waiting a few more minutes (I am really starting to get hungry), our waitress finally showed up.

OMG!

Wow…wow…wow! Stephanie Keller finally came over to our table to say hello and get our drink orders. OMG! She was blonde, really athletic looking, and soooooooooo cute. But what really impressed me was her outgoing personality. Like I said…wow.

When I was single, I remember meeting some girls who were really good looking, but as soon as they would open their mouth to talk, their "hotness" would disappear. For some reason, hearing them talk would ruin it for me. I guess I would compare it to some of the reality shows you see on TV. When you watch these shows for the first time, you will probably notice a few people who might be absolutely gorgeous. TV producers aren't stupid. They do this for a reason. Attractive people get viewers' attention, which ultimately leads to higher ratings. However, when I hear some of these beautiful people talk, it's like nails on a chalkboard for me. Please shut up! Please stop talking! It's making you ugly!

Stephanie, on the other hand, was the real deal. She was very bubbly, confident, and even wanted to talk sports with me. Unbelievable! After we finished eating, I asked my dad if he could get lost for a few minutes. Please go to the bathroom ~~or go befriend another waitress in case this doesn't work out~~. Thankfully, my dad actually listened to me this time and left the table for a few minutes. Later on, when I glanced around the restaurant to see where my dad went, I saw him at the bar having a friendly conversation with some homeless-looking dude. What a great wingman!

While my dad was making a new friend, I was able to talk to Stephanie by myself for a few minutes when she came back to the table with our bill. Again, she had the most amazing personality. She came across as the coolest girl ever. Did I mention she talked sports with me?

While she was talking, I was doing my best to think of how I could ask for her phone number. I was not exactly Casanova back then. I was typically too nervous, too scared of rejection, or too whatever to ask a girl for her number or out on a date. However, I definitely wanted to see this girl again and needed to quickly figure out a "cool" way to ask for her number. The best I could do was say in a funny, sarcastic tone, "Sooooo… are you going to give me your phone number?" (That is so bad!)

Stephanie responded with a sassy, "Do you *want* my phone number?"

Yes, please!

To my surprise, she then wrote a phone number on my receipt. Now I was just praying it was actually her phone number and not some random one she made up. The good thing was the number she wrote down had ten digits to it, although I did not recognize the area code.

> ***While On the Subject:*** A few months earlier, I had met an attractive girl who was helping me pick out some new eyeglasses at a store. She had been flirting with me (I thought), and when I paid for my glasses, she wrote on my receipt her name with a smiley face beside it and a phone number. She gave me her phone number (I thought) without me even asking for it! It absolutely made my day and gave me a big boost of confidence. However, when I called that phone number the next day, I got the LensCrafters corporate office.

I was hoping this would not happen to me a second time. The next day, I called the number, and thankfully, Stephanie had given me her *actual* phone number! I was ecstatic when I heard Stephanie answer the phone instead of a customer service representative. I was even more excited when she agreed to go out on a date with me the following night. Needless to say, our first date was pretty memorable.

First Date

To this day, I can be guilty of being ~~cheap~~ frugal. I am always looking for ways to save money or get a good deal. However, in my early twenties, I would do pretty much anything short of giving a kidney to save a buck. I would take a survey, sign up for a credit card, be in a focus group, taste-test food, or test-drive a car if it meant getting something free.

A few days before meeting Stephanie, I had received two free movie tickets to see *Men in Black II* after participating in a marketing promotion at the mall. Like normal, I was planning to go see the movie by myself (kind of sad). However, since I had these free tickets, I could see if Stephanie would want to go with me. This would be an easy way for me to ask her out on a date AND not spend any money!

This would be a win-win! If I found out on the date she was a terrible human being, I would only have wasted my time and not my money (since I didn't have much of it).

I am so fortunate Stephanie agreed to go see the movie with me, especially when my lack of charm almost screwed it up. On the phone, I actually told her I had won two free movie tickets and didn't have anyone to go see it with.

I mean…how could anyone say no to that?

Looking back, you can tell I was a complete amateur when it came to dating. I had ONE CHANCE to make a good impression on this beautiful girl. Where should I take her to try to impress her and show her how much fun of a person I could be? How about I take her to the movies WHERE YOU ARE NOT ALLOWED TO TALK! If we hit it off on this first date, maybe I could take her to the library the following weekend. (*THINK*, KEVIN!)

I am also just flabbergasted at how I was more concerned about saving money than I was about making Stephanie feel special. (Stupid!)

On the phone, Stephanie told me she would prefer to pick me up instead of vice versa. Being naive, I didn't know why she wouldn't just let me be a gentleman and pick her up. However, Stephanie was being smart and providing herself a way of escape if the date did not go well. She also did not want a stranger to know where she lived, in case I ended up being a complete jerk. (Apparently, she had been on a few bad dates before.)

When I opened my apartment door that night and saw Stephanie, my jaw dropped. I had initially thought she was really cute when we first met at Hooters. However, outside of work, she was GORGEOUS! I know that sounds weird since she was in her Hooters uniform when we first met.

I felt like I had just won the lottery by being able to go on one date with a Hooters girl. Unfortunately, I didn't exactly know how to act around pretty girls. Not only did I NOT spend any money on her during that first date, but I also asked her if she was on one of those Hooters calendars. If so, I was going to see if she could autograph one for me. (Dumb!)

I assumed this date would only be a one-time thing. First off, based on looks alone, she was way out of my league (just ask my dad). Second, I was a *very* conservative guy, *very* naive, and a little socially awkward. So I assumed she was not going to like me.

During our date, I remember having fun but not exactly hitting it off. On the way back to my apartment after the movie, Stephanie asked if it bothered me that she worked at Hooters. Kind of a gutsy question on a first date, don't you think?

Of course, it didn't bother me that she worked at Hooters. As you can tell, I was actually quite proud to be going out on a date with a Hooters girl (i.e., I almost asked her for her autograph!).

However, I interpreted her question as, "If we were dating, would it bother you that I work at Hooters?"

I responded with a matter-of-fact "yes" (so hypocritical!). She then explained how she became a waitress at Hooters (coworker from one of her other jobs) and why she was working there (to pay for nursing school). In the nicest way possible, she told me to be careful about judging a book by its cover. I shouldn't make such a hard opinion of her solely on the fact that she was working at Hooters.

After that fun little exchange, I was thinking there definitely was not going to be a second date. When Stephanie pulled her car into a parking spot in front of my apartment, I thought I would be nice and invite her inside to hang out. I expected her to say no thanks, give me a phony hug, and then never see her again. But like usual, things did not go as I expected.

She actually said yes to my invitation to hang out a little bit longer. I was shocked she actually wanted to spend a little bit more time with me. Once inside my dirty apartment, we had a conversation I will never forget.

Me:	"I'll be honest with you, I was really nervous about meeting you the other night. My dad tried to set me up one other time, and it was kind of a train wreck. I had agreed to meet with one of his coworkers' daughters. Unfortunately, this girl had dropped out of high school, was living with her parents, and had just had a baby. I remember thinking, 'I thought my dad had a higher opinion of me than this!'" (Silence)
Stephanie:	"Sooooo...this might be a good time to tell you about my daughter."
Me:	"Daughter?" (*ARE YOU KIDDING ME! This night keeps getting better!*)
Stephanie:	"Yes, daughter."
Me:	"From a previous boyfriend?"
Stephanie:	"No, from a previous marriage." (*You're probably only twenty-one or twenty-two years old... and you've already been married, had a kid, AND gone through a divorce! WAIT...ARE YOU DIVORCED?*)
Me:	(Trying not to look or sound flustered.) "Uh...what is your daughter's name?"
Stephanie:	"Sha-nay-nay"
Me:	"Wait. What?"
Stephanie:	(Laughing) "I am TOTALLY teasing you! I don't have any kids." (I immediately fell over on the couch in disbelief and busted out laughing.)
Stephanie:	"THAT is what you get for being so uptight about everything tonight!"

I absolutely laughed my rear end off! She completely pulled one on me and I TOTALLY deserved it. Her prank completely broke the ice for me. After I finally stopped laughing and eventually caught my breath, we had such a fun conversation.

Wow. This girl was amazing. This girl was different. This girl was like a unicorn!

Sorry folks, I do not have any pictures to share from when we met ~~at Denny's~~.

CHAPTER 2

THE PROPOSAL

My Biggest Fear

As a young adult trying to navigate life, I had a lot of fears and insecurities. Fear of failing. Fear of not being good enough. Fear of getting fired. Was I smart enough to pass the CPA exam? Could I be good enough to have a professional career?

However, the thing that scared me the most was the idea of getting married. Divorce had been rampant in my family, along with what appeared to be some unhappily married folks too. Seeing unhappy people stay together for the kids...or because they felt stuck...or for financial reasons...or for whatever, didn't exactly motivate me to rush to the altar. But the primary source of my fear was from the hurt I experienced from my own parents' divorce.

After twenty-seven years of marriage, my parents made the life-altering decision to end their holy matrimony. Even though I was an adult when it happened, at the age of twenty-one, their divorce changed my life. And not in a good way.

For a few years after my parents had separated and then divorced, talking about my family was a sensitive subject for me. It was pretty much off limits to talk about. Too painful. For example, I remember going out to dinner one night with Stephanie after we had just started dating. She was asking me a bunch of questions about my background and where I grew up and then eventually about my family. As you might expect, I didn't want to talk about my family. However, if this beautiful woman was wanting to get to know me on a more personal level...I thought I should probably try to open up a little bit.

Unfortunately, not long after I began telling her about my family, I started to get emotional. I then politely excused myself from the table so she wouldn't see me in a vulnerable state. I walked out of the restaurant, sat down on a bench, and tried to compose myself. By that time, I had met Stephanie's family and had gotten to see how they interacted with each other. I saw the closeness she had with her parents and her siblings. They were the kind of family I *used* to have.

I saw the Keller's go shopping together, go to dinner together, tell stories, laugh at each other, have fun just hanging out as a family, and then give genuine love-filled hugs when they had to leave each other. Seeing that actually made me sad. It made me sad because I could no longer experience that with my own family. Those days were long gone. A distant memory.

I had someone recently, who knew my parents years ago, ask me whose fault I thought the divorce was. My response was, "Don't know. Don't care." Too many layers to peel. It happened. It's over. The damage has been done.

Fellow pastors and ministers tried to help. A psychologist tried to help. Family members tried to help. Church members tried to help. It was complicated.

Hands down, my parents divorce was the single, most hurtful thing I have ever experienced in my life. It was devastating to me, my immediate family, and a couple hundred church members. Not to even mention the impact it would have on a future generation of grandchildren.

Sadly, I have found out that time does not heal all wounds. I am convinced only God can. Although that divorce took place twenty years ago, my family has never recovered. This is really sad, but I can't even remember the last time we were all in the same room...at the same time. It may have been at my Uncle Fred's funeral a few years ago. Maybe it was at my wedding back in 2004. I honestly don't know.

I realize I didn't *physically* lose my parents or siblings to that divorce, but I did lose my family. And because of that painful experience, I didn't believe getting married was worth the risk. Thankfully, my perspective of marriage, family, and church would only be temporarily damaged.

Ring or Motorcycle?

When I met Stephanie in July 2002, I was obviously not thinking about marriage. However, I do remember thinking she was more fun to hang around with than anyone I had ever met. After dating for around two or three months, I set up a separate savings account and started shifting money to it from each biweekly paycheck, in case our relationship got serious. Although I was scared to death about the idea of getting married, I wanted to make sure I was financially prepared if I ever changed my mind. If, by some long shot, Stephanie ended up being "the one," this savings account would ensure I had some money to buy her a nice engagement ring or at least put a big down payment toward one. On the flip side, if things didn't work out, I would have the money to buy a motorcycle. THAT is what you call a win-win!

Spoiler alert: I didn't get the motorcycle.

I Am Shocked Stephanie Didn't Break Up with Me

After fifteen years of marriage and over two years of dating, I still think it is pretty amazing we ended up together. When we met, I was clueless about so many things. My view of what marriage should look like was dysfunctional and my behavior, at times, was cringeworthy. Should I go on?

I am shocked Stephanie didn't break up with me. However, I should never have reminded her of this.

To celebrate our fourteenth anniversary, we decided to go to a high-end steakhouse called "The Barn" in New Albany, Ohio ~~because I had a gift card~~. While waiting for the meal, our conversation turned to reminiscing about the past. We were both so thankful for our marriage, our family, and for what God had done in our lives. But the conversation ended up going in a very different direction than I expected (as usual). I'll give you my best play-by-play version of how this conversation went.

Me:	"Looking back to when we first met, it is pretty amazing we ended up together. I am shocked you didn't break up with me at some point during the…" (Before I could even finish my sentence, my wife interrupted me.)
Stephanie:	"OH MY GOSH! I think about that all the time! I am shocked I didn't break up with you either!" (My mouth was now open…pretty surprised by what I just heard.)
Me:	"Wait…what?!"
Stephanie:	(Now laughing.) "I am SO SORRY! Oh my goodness!" (Stephanie started to laugh even harder after seeing my facial reaction.)
Me:	"Okayyyy! When I made that statement a few seconds ago, I thought one of two things might happen. And your response was NEITHER of those."
Stephanie:	"COME ON NOW!" (Doing a terrible job of trying to control her laughter.)
Me:	"I was NOT expecting you to finish my sentence! I thought there might be an awkward silence if you actually agreed with me." (My wife busted out laughing even harder now. Other tables were starting to look at us.)

Me:	"OR...I thought you might say something like 'Oh no, honey! Breaking up with you NEVER even crossed my mind. You may have been a little socially awkward, but I knew you had the potential to turn into an AMAZING man if you hung around me a little bit.'"
Stephanie:	(Trying to catch her breath.) "I'm so, SO SORRY! Yes, that would have been a better response! But let's be honest here...you know it HAD to be God!"
	(My wife started laughing at herself now, thinking she was funny.)
Stephanie:	"Am I right? Or am I right!"

She was not funny.

Stephanie now had a case of the giggles and could not stop laughing. She was trying to catch her breath but continued to laugh out loud. Multiple tables started looking at us, but it didn't bother me at all. It was our anniversary and my wife was having fun. I love it when I can make her laugh, even when it is at my expense.

I Need a Sign

Although I wanted to fall in love and live a life that looked straight out of a movie, I didn't know if I could ever get past my fear of divorce. For me to get married, I pretty much needed to audibly hear God yell at me (in a James Earl Jones type of voice), "KEVIN RONALD MASON! The guy with social security number XXX–XX–XXXX! This is GOD! I brought Stephanie Ann Keller into your life. Marry that woman!"

While we were dating, I constantly struggled with the idea of possibly getting married, so much, in fact, that I was concerned I might be wasting Stephanie's time. It reminds me of when I was younger, playing cards with one of my cousins who would yell out, "Either crap or get off the pot!" He would always yell this at anyone who took too long of a turn. I was now the person taking too long to make a decision. We had been dating for a year and a half, and I was still not mentally ready to get married…even to a unicorn.

Like so many other things I have done, this one sounds really stupid to me now. I remember asking God to give me a sign if Stephanie was "the one" I was supposed to marry. In my mind, this was just too big of a decision for me to make without getting some type of divine confirmation from heaven. While driving to Stephanie's apartment one day, I prayed to God if He wanted me to marry Stephanie Keller, then please have an elephant walk across the road in front of me right then.

That didn't work.

"Okay, God. How about you have *any* type of zoo animal run across the road…NOW!"

Nothing.

"Okay. Not now…NOW!"

Nothing.

The Sign

About a week later, I got a sign. Thankfully, it did not involve me potentially hitting any zoo animals with my car. I decided to reach out to a family friend and mentor of mine to ask him a few questions. Bishop Courtney McBath had met Stephanie a few months earlier when we had visited with him in Cincinnati. He seemed like the best person to speak with about relationships, especially since he had written a book titled *Maximize Your Marriage.* I sent him an email and briefly explained how I was struggling to make a decision of whether or not I should propose to Stephanie.

The next morning, I opened my email to see his response. It read something like this:

"Kevin, you are an idiot if you do not marry that girl."

If Bill Engvall had been with me, he would have said, "Here's your sign!"

How You Propose Matters

That email actually did it for me. That was the confirmation I needed to mentally get me over the hump. I was now 100% certain I was going to propose. No turning back.

Now I just needed to figure out a way to propose that would surprise Stephanie, be memorable, and give her a story she would be proud to share. The women I knew who had gotten engaged were always SOOOOO excited to tell the world. They would show off their new bling to everyone, ~~whether you cared or not~~. As a single guy, I would always play nice and act like I cared. Sometimes I would even try to complement their ring, although I knew nothing about what I was looking at. My response would be something like, "That is gorgeous. It's round!" However, I couldn't tell if I was looking at a diamond or a birthstone. Nor could I tell if you bought it from Kay the jeweler or from Kay the crack dealer.

Then someone would inevitably ask the bride-to-be, "Sooo…how did he propose?" This was always fascinating to me. Every now and then, I would hear a crazy, over-the-top romantic story ~~and then throw up in my mouth a little bit~~. Other times, I might hear a REALLY bad one ~~and laugh my rear end off after walking away~~.

My favorite bad proposal story is from someone I used to work with in public accounting. After a shopping trip to the mall, my coworker was walking back to the car when her boyfriend said, "Hey, what's beside that tire over there?" He then reached under some random car and acted like he found a ring behind the tire (which also just happened to be her size). After "magically" finding this diamond engagement ring underneath a car, he spun around on one knee and proposed to her inside the parking garage. (This guy was even more clueless than I was!) She immediately declined his proposal and told him he needed to do better than that.

Good for her. She had standards! Of course, she told this story to us *after* she had accepted his second round of proposals. Unfortunately, I didn't hear what he came up with for an encore because I couldn't get past the first attempt. For all I know, he proposed at a nice truck stop somewhere in Virginia. (The state slogan is "Virginia is for lovers!")

I will refrain from sharing anymore bad proposal stories because the other ones I am thinking of are from people I still know. I assume they will read this book at some point, and I would hate to ~~hear from them~~ embarrass them in any way. However, hearing these stories taught me *how* you propose matters.

Asking Permission

Before proposing to Stephanie, I wanted to get her parents' blessing. It was important to me that I get approval from *both* of them if possible. I knew I wasn't just going to be marrying Stephanie. I would be marrying Stephanie AND her family. I called her dad, Steve, and asked if he and Brenda could meet me somewhere to talk. We decided on the McDonald's in Bellefontaine, Ohio, which was close to the midway point between Columbus and her hometown. It would be about an hour-and-fifteen-minute drive, which would give me enough time to think, pray, and rehearse what I was going to say. After doing all that, I would pray some more and then take some deep breaths.

I felt I had a pretty good relationship with Steve and anticipated him welcoming me into the family with open arms. However, I wasn't so sure about her mother, Brenda. I was not very astute at reading people (i.e., LensCrafters girl). Back then, I actually thought Brenda didn't like me. I think I got this impression from the times when she would playfully yell at me and act like I was kind of annoying her. I failed to notice how she would playfully do the same thing to her husband and son. I didn't realize this was kind of her unique way of accepting me.

Apparently, I had nothing to be concerned about. I found out years later that on their way home from meeting me for the very first time, Brenda had told Steve she thought I would marry their daughter someday. That was news to me since the only thing I remember from that first meeting was Stephanie's entire family making fun of me for never having seen *Star Wars*.

I wasn't sure what reaction I would get when I pulled into that McDonald's parking lot. I could see through the window that Steve and

Brenda were already there, drinking coffee and waiting to ~~interrogate me~~ speak with me. I think we had some small talk for about thirty seconds before I started reciting the lines I had rehearsed in the car about fifty times. Then I pulled out a box from my coat pocket to show them the ring I had purchased with my ~~motorcycle~~ savings.

Brenda was shocked when she saw the ring. Thank God it was a "that is beautiful" kind of reaction instead of an "I am embarrassed for you" kind of reaction. I also remember getting a priceless reaction from my soon-to-be father-in-law.

Steve: "Whoa! Brenda, would you look at THAT! I *TOLD* you
             he would eventually come around!"
Brenda: "I'll admit it…I had my doubts."

I did too!

I was so relieved when they *both* gave me their blessing and said they would be honored to have me as part of their family. Not only did I hit the jackpot with my wife, but I definitely won the lottery with the Keller family. Amazing in-laws. Phenomenal grandparents. Great Christmas gift givers!

I Almost Ran Out of Time

I bought Stephanie's engagement ring on Valentine's Day in 2004 but did not propose to her until almost mid-April. Those two months felt like two years. To be able to surprise Stephanie, I had to do my best to hide the ring *and* hide my true feelings. By this time, I had learned that Stephanie is REALLY hard to surprise. I have only been able to do it a handful of times in the seventeen years I have known her. In my attempt to surprise her, I almost ran out of time.

By the first week of April, Stephanie had been offered a traveling RN position somewhere in California. I know it was a very tempting opportunity for her and sounded kind of exciting. Guess what was the only thing holding her back from pursuing this career path? Yeah, that's right...me.

While she was considering this opportunity, Stephanie wanted to know what was going on with us. Thankfully, she didn't want to make a career decision until she spoke to me about what I thought our future together might look like. She just straight up asked me if I saw a long-term future with her. (You know, either crap or get off the pot!) I think she was wanting to get some type of relationship commitment from me at that moment, but I was in actor mode. I had already fully committed myself to playing the role of a disinterested boyfriend. After almost seven weeks in this role, I couldn't break character, especially since I was so close to the finish line! Now I really had to develop some acting chops to somehow convince Stephanie to turn down this career opportunity for a chance at a lifetime of happiness with me.

I told her I was not ready to make any type of long-term commitment yet but agreed to start researching and possibly even looking at engagement rings with her. Fortunately, my promise to start researching rings was enough to convince her to stick around Columbus a little bit longer. I thought that was going to be the final hurdle I would face before proposing. Again, I would be wrong.

Another Good Trick

My plan was to propose over Easter weekend that year (Google is showing the date as Saturday, April 10, 2004). The Thursday night before proposing (less than two days before popping the question), my sneaky wife-to-be pulled another one on me.

After dinner at my apartment:

Stephanie: "I am curious. Were you really serious last week when you said you would be open to the idea of looking at engagement rings?"

Me: (Still in actor mode.) "Absolutely. I am open to looking, but that's it."

Stephanie:	"Thank you! Thank you! Thank you!"
Me:	"Why?"
Stephanie:	"Because you have an appointment tomorrow night at The Diamond Cellar. You need to be there at 5:30. Ask for Jeff." (Trying not to break character...but my mouth was open and I was kind of in shock/panic mode.)
Stephanie:	"There it is! SEE!"
Me:	"See what?"
Stephanie:	"Your reaction! I knew you weren't serious about looking at rings!" (Stephanie was now bursting into tears.)
Me:	"I'm confused. Do I or do I NOT have an appointment tomorrow?"
Stephanie:	"No! I just made that up to see if you were serious about marrying me or not. I was testing you." (I felt absolutely TERRIBLE. I was now sick to my stomach because I could not tell her my secret yet.)
Stephanie:	(~~Over-the-top dramatic~~ slightly emotional.) "AND YOU FAILED!"

I only needed to hold onto my secret for another thirty-eight hours. That was *another* good trick she pulled on me! Do all single ladies play these games with their boyfriends?

(On the positive side, I was REALLY getting good at this acting thing. For someone who has never taken an acting class, I felt like I really nailed the role of playing myself.)

The Proposal

Stephanie is really close with her family, so I wanted to somehow include them in the marriage proposal. I chose the Saturday of Easter weekend to propose because it would be the next time her entire family would be together. The Keller family had a lot of fun traditions with holidays (and vacations). I had learned their Easter traditions included giving their adult children an Easter basket and then having an overly competitive Easter egg hunt.

Those egg hunts were TOUGH! Brenda would hide the eggs inside cereal boxes, on top of kitchen cabinets, in between couch cushions, and so on. I never stood a chance at this game. It was funny, though, to watch my future wife, brother-in-law, and sister-in-law tear apart their parents' house just to find some M&Ms.

Unfortunately, this tradition died when the grandkids came along. Now, Grandma Brenda just throws a bunch of eggs out in the backyard for the grandkids "to find." (Brenda, you got soft!)

I thought I might be able to surprise Stephanie if I combined a marriage proposal with one of her family traditions. However, I would need help with a few of the details such as:

1. Getting Stephanie away from her parents' house so I could show up and hide.
2. Figuring out a way to hide my car so Stephanie wouldn't see it.
3. Trying to video record the moment.
4. Ensuring Stephanie would NOT be wearing her normal Saturday attire (workout clothes, ponytail, and no makeup).

Since we were going to attempt to record the proposal, I didn't want Stephanie to possibly watch the video later and hate it because of not having any makeup on or being dressed down during that special moment. Like the great mother she is, Brenda solved these problems like a champ.

1. She told her son, Steven, he was going to have to drive an hour out of his way to come pick me up on his way home for Easter. She told him I would be coming home that weekend to surprise Stephanie and was warned to NOT say a word to either of his sisters.
2. On that Saturday morning, Brenda told Stephanie she needed to go run an errand with her dad. That errand ended up being going to the grocery store and car wash to kill some time.

3. She told Steve he was going to videotape the kids' Easter baskets.

4. When Brenda saw what Stephanie was wearing to go to the grocery store, she made her change clothes. She said something like, "Why don't you make yourself look presentable one time this weekend!"

All four of these are just hilarious to me. NOBODY questioned Mom when she told them what to do, which is exactly how it should be!

As his mother had ordered, my future brother-in-law picked me up at my apartment around 9:00 that Saturday morning. I think Steven was looking forward to spending some guy time with me that morning because he talked my ear off the *entire* two-hour trip. As he was telling me about something important to him, I remember looking out the window and wanting to throw up. I was nervous. I was excited. I was scared. This felt like the biggest moment of my life. I love Steven and tried my best to be polite, but I wasn't paying attention to whatever he was saying. My mind was elsewhere.

We stopped at a gas station a few miles from the Keller house, and Steven called his mom. We obviously did not want to pull in the driveway if Stephanie was still around. I am glad we called because Stephanie was still at the house (probably trying to figure out what she was supposed to wear to the grocery store). Since she had not left the house yet, this meant I had more guy time with Steven…sitting in his car…waiting for Stephanie to leave…to help her dad pick out a box of cereal.

Once Brenda called us back to confirm they had left, we drove to the house and I hid in their basement office. I locked the door and stayed there until it was time to pop the question. After an hour or so of reading the newspaper and playing solitaire on their computer, Brenda unlocked the door and informed me that Katie (my soon-to-be sister-in-law) was home and Steve had just pulled in the driveway with Steph. She would have them open their Easter baskets as soon as everyone got inside.

My proposal plan was to put three pictures in Stephanie's Easter basket. The first picture was of me on my knee with the caption, "Steph, will you marry me?" The second picture was of her ring. The third was of me in front of a Hooters billboard that read, "638 days later…Steph, will you marry me?"

While On the Subject: I had the third picture taken by my buddy, Paul, in front of the Hooters restaurant where we had met. I called the restaurant manager and asked if I could use their billboard to help me propose to one of their former waitresses. He actually remembered Stephanie and was happy to oblige, but only if I did it before the restaurant opened and promised to put the sign back to whatever NASCAR message was up there. So Paul and I went to the restaurant early one Saturday morning to take a few pictures. While he was trying to take my picture, numerous cars started honking their horns at us to either cheer me on...or mock me. Paul got really embarrassed and just started clicking away on the camera without me knowing. After a brief moment, I told him to tell me when he was ready so I could smile. He then informed me he had already taken about thirty pictures. He just wanted to get out of there ASAP because of all the commotion going on around us. Thankfully, we were able to get one good picture I could use.

After Stephanie saw these three pictures in her basket, the plan was for her to call me with her answer. Then once my cell phone rang, I would walk upstairs, get down on my knee, and propose in front of her family. That was the plan. I'll let Stephanie share with you how it went.

Spoiler alert: I *CRUSHED* it!

Memory of Proposal
(Written by Stephanie Mason)

It was like any other Saturday morning at my parents' house. My dad and I got up to work out and then had breakfast. I showered and put on some comfy, cozy clothes for the day. When I went upstairs, my mom just looked at me. "Stephanie, can you please put on nicer clothes than that, do your hair, and put on some makeup? I need some things and want you to go with your dad." As usual, I did what I was told and didn't question

Mom. After I made my appearance more appropriate, my dad and I left to run some errands for Mom.

We got home about an hour and a half later, and it was immediately time to open our Easter baskets, which was different from our normal tradition. I also noticed something else different as Mom decided to pick the order of how we would open our baskets. Even though this was different from prior years, I didn't think anything of it.

I noticed a large manila envelope in each of our baskets and was curious what these were for. My older brother went first, and when he opened his envelope, there were several 8×10 pictures of him as a child. Since my parents were now empty nesters, I thought they were getting sentimental by giving us some pictures and video-recording us opening these baskets. Then my mom told my younger sister, Katie, it was her turn. Her basket also included an envelope with pictures of her as a child. Then it was my turn.

I looked in my basket and saw some candy and the manila envelope. My mom reminded me to look at each picture in the order they were in and then show the camera. The first picture was of me when I was maybe two years old. Everyone "oohed and ahhed" as I held it up to the camera. Then I looked down at my next picture and it took my breath away.

In the picture, Kevin was kneeling on one knee while holding a ring with the caption, "Steph, will you marry me?" My jaw dropped and my hand immediately covered my mouth. I was both shocked and speechless. Katie came over to look at the picture and immediately started screaming. As Katie continued to scream in excitement, she started running around the house and hugging everyone in the room. Then she began jumping up and down on the furniture. I then flipped to the next picture and it was a picture of the ring. MY ring!

Then I looked at the final picture, which showed Kevin in front of the Hooters restaurant where we had met. On the sign, he had the exact number of days since we had met and asked if I would marry him. My hand was still over my mouth in shock, while my sister was still running around the house in shock and screaming. Mom handed me the phone and told me I was supposed to call Kevin with my answer.

When I tried calling his cell phone, it just kept ringing and ringing before finally going to his voicemail. I was so sad because I could not give him my answer or talk to him. My brother grabbed the phone and tried to call him again. I assumed he was in the middle of his tournament and would just call me whenever his softball game was over. I started to look at the pictures again and then I heard someone coming up the stairs.

Then my sister started yelling, "It's Kevin! It's Kevin! It's Kevin!" I think I lost all feeling in my body at that moment. It is VERY hard to surprise me and my soon-to-be fiancé just did it twice in a matter of seconds! Kevin came up the stairs, walked around the couch, his eyes focused on me the entire time, dropped to one knee, and proposed in front of my entire family. Wow.

Initially, I didn't give him an answer. All I could say was "NO, YOU DIDN'T!" because I was in complete shock. My dad continued to videotape and provide his play-by-play commentary of the moment while my brother sat on the couch, watching the drama unfold like a spectator. Then my sister would not stop screaming and dancing all through the house while my mom started to cry. I would be the first of their three children to get married.

I eventually told Kevin, "YES!" so he could put the ring on my finger, but I remember not wanting to stop hugging him. I was so, so, so excited!

America's Funniest Home Video?

I am not going to lie…the video of me proposing to Stephanie is, hands down, one of the funniest things I have ever seen. Describing Katie's reaction to me proposing to her sister does NOT do it justice. She dang near lost her mind as she was jumping on the couch, running across the room, yelling, dancing by herself, hugging her mother, screaming, and hugging Stephanie and me. We watched it on our anniversary this past year, and I am sooooo glad we were able to capture that moment on camera. I had not seen the DVD for several years, but after watching it again, that video is even better than I remembered. We actually thought about sending it to *America's Funniest Home Videos* but never did. It is not a quick five-second clip like most of the videos on that show, so I am not sure AFV would even show it.

Right before our wedding, we played a few minutes of the video for everyone to see. The reactions from our guests were priceless as we heard a loud roar of laughter coming from inside the church. Unfortunately, my new sister-in-law did not find this video as funny as everyone else. Katie told us later on that she had people coming up to her during the entire reception to tell her how funny she was. I guess all the attention was a little embarrassing for her and her boyfriend (now husband). However, it will be fun for Uncle Kevin to show that video to her two sons when they are a little bit older.

You can view our proposal video by going to www.kevinandsteph.com.

A First Time for Everything

Our wedding ~~night~~ could not get here soon enough. During our six-month engagement, we planned a wedding, decided to build a new house, Stephanie started a new job, and I became ~~homeless~~ domestically challenged. Let's just say, it was a *rough* six months.

To anyone reading this, I would NOT recommend trying to do all these big life events at the same time. Just one of these is stressful enough, let alone being ambitious and taking them all on. We definitely had a few things to learn. This led to a few moments where we felt incredibly overwhelmed with everything we were trying to accomplish. I now realize that most of this self-inflicted stress was due to our lack of life experience. Even though these six months were incredibly challenging for us, it was the first time Stephanie and I had to trust God together.

It would not be the last.

Surprisingly, it took about 30 pictures for me to finally get this right.
"Your tie is crooked… you are not centered on the fireplace…
you need to hold the ring completely flat… why aren't you smiling?"

Here is the ring I bought with my
~~motorcycle~~ savings.

This might be my best picture of all time!

CHAPTER 3

Marriage

What NOT to Do When You Get Married

Poor Stephanie. She now had to live with me. I had no clue how to be a good husband or how to meet my wife's emotional needs. I was actually planning to write a chapter about what NOT to do when you get married. However, after instantly thinking of multiple stories I could share off the top of my head, I might be able to write an entire book on this topic alone (depending on how this one goes). Our first few months of marriage were a comedy of errors.

I told Stephanie my idea of potentially writing a book on this topic down the road and she responded with a straight face, "That is probably going to be a REALLY long book."

I also mistakenly mentioned this idea to my in-laws during a recent family dinner. My mother-in-law immediately started rattling off her list of stupid stuff she has seen me do over the past seventeen years. I had to politely interrupt and let her know she could give me her list of grievances *after* I finished this book.

Not a Marriage Guru

Unfortunately, after taking a few weeks of premarital counseling, I was still a complete idiot when it came to marriage. Although we had dated for over two years, we had never lived together and still had a lot to learn about each other. For me, it was kind of like when you become a first-time parent. You can read all the books and articles you want, but you really don't know what life is going to be like as a parent. It doesn't really kick in until you hold that baby for the first time and then no longer sleep more than two to three continuous hours at a time. That was also what marriage was like for me. I did some homework on the topic, but it really didn't make much sense…until *after* we got married.

> ***While On the Subject:*** Here is one of my favorite quotes from Stephanie. She ~~yelled~~ politely said this to me in an ~~annoyed/irritated/slightly enraged~~ angelic tone about a week after delivering a baby.
>
>   *"How can you possibly be tired?! You got, like, four hours of sleep…IN A ROW!"*
>
> That was a great point, honey. I mean, how could I *possibly* have been tired?

A Week of Firsts
(Written by Stephanie Mason)

I just shake my head thinking about our honeymoon. That was a week of many firsts for Kevin, including his first alcoholic beverage. He was twenty-six years old and had never tasted a beer, had a mixed drink, or drank a shot. That was certainly NOT a bad thing. However, it is very rare in this world for a guy like him to have gone through all of high school and college, been a part of so many sports teams, attended various corporate parties and events…and to have NEVER taken a sip. That takes some incredible discipline. That is also very admirable, in my opinion.

However, since the drinks at our all-inclusive resort were free, Kevin decided to use that week to experiment. It was hilarious to watch my new husband taste-test a bunch of random drinks like a teenager. He quickly found out the only drinks he liked were the piña coladas and strawberry daiquiris. After seeing him double-fisting those back to our pool chairs, I unfortunately had to be the bearer of bad news. To protect him from getting publicly ridiculed someday, I told him he should NEVER order any of these drinks at a corporate party, happy hour, or anywhere near one of my relatives.

Just One Story

I changed my mind…I'll give you one story.

As you can probably tell by now, my wife has been a bad influence on me, starting with our honeymoon. I used to be such a good, wholesome guy…and then I got married. (Steph, I am kidding!)

For our honeymoon, we went to an all-inclusive resort in Riviera Maya, Mexico (I can't remember the name of it). During that week, we made reservations to go to their top-rated restaurant onsite. I was excited to experience what real, authentic, non-Americanized Mexican food would taste like. I was told it was going to be a lot different than Taco Bell. ("Uh…excuse me, señor. What do you mean you don't have any Doritos Gordita Crunch Tacos?!")

Before I even got to taste the food, I ran into a problem. Our server came to the table and asked if we were at the resort celebrating anything. We told him we had just gotten married and were on our honeymoon. He was like, "Congratulations! I bring you surprise!" I thought he might bring us some fried ice cream like I had gotten as a kid on my birthday at Chi-Chi's. I loved that fried ice cream! Again, I was wrong.

A couple of minutes went by before our server came back to our table with two shots that were on fire! My heart sank. That was the complete opposite of fried ice cream. I immediately tried to change his mind because I did not want to take a shot. However, I couldn't tell this nice guy, who barely spoke English, that I wasn't a drinker or that my parents taught me I would go straight to hell if I drank this devil juice. I thought that message might get lost in translation. So I waved my hands and said, "No, no, no…you don't have to do that! We don't need to do any shots here."

He either didn't understand me OR was just ignoring me. Our server then turned this into the ultimate peer pressure moment for me when he began yelling throughout the restaurant, "EVERYONE! ATTENTION! THIS IS KEVIN AND STEPHANIE! THEY ON HONEYMOON!"

He then motioned for Stephanie to drink up. Ladies first. My new bride blew out the fire, chugged that shot like a champ, and then slammed the glass down on the table. (Apparently, she had done this before. SINNER!) The entire restaurant erupted in cheers while our server high-fived Steph and celebrated like she had just scored a goal or something.

I thought, *OMG…my brand new wife is going to hell!*

If you could only have seen the look on my face at that moment, I was absolutely stunned. I had no idea she could drink a shot like that! My jaw just dropped. I could NOT believe what I just saw! Did I just see that? I thought we were on our honeymoon. This just turned into spring break!

The server then looked at me and yelled out, "NOW, MAN!"

That was my cue to attempt to chug this flaming whatever, for the first time in my life, in front of a cheering audience. So I then did my absolute best to copy exactly what my wife just did.

Blow out the flame. Put the shot glass up to my mouth. Tip it back. Swallow the entire warm, chocolate, cough syrup-tasting drink all at once. Slam the glass down.

COUGH!

HACK!

GAG!

SOMETHING WENT DOWN THE WRONG PIPE!

MORE COUGHING!

WHY ISN'T ANYONE HELPING ME?!

MORE HACKING!

NOW HITTING MY CHEST WITH FIST!

The entire restaurant erupted in laughter. Nobody even tried to help me! My new bride (the boozer) didn't offer me water OR a pat on the back OR the Heimlich OR any other type of medical assistance! Isn't she supposed to be a nurse?!

Instead, she could not stop laughing or high-fiving everyone around her. Our server, now a comedian, hilariously raised my wife's hand and yelled across the restaurant, "WINNER!"

Needless to say, that was the first *and* last shot I ever drank.

Poor Stephanie.
She now had to live with me.

Kids, this was my friend, Micah's, car. We did
not take an Uber to our wedding reception.

The night of my first and last shot on our honeymoon.

CHAPTER 4

THE ELECTROCUTION

*Unless noted otherwise, this chapter was written by Stephanie Mason.

The Operating Room

After getting married, we talked about Kevin going back to school at some point to help with advancing his career. I had been a registered nurse for three years, loved it, and had no intention of ever going back to school. However, there was a hospital in town that would pay for half of your family member's tuition if you worked there a certain amount of time. This would include tuition toward a master's degree program if they were to attend the university associated with the hospital. At that time, the cost of the MBA program at this university was around $40,000 (and I am sure much higher today). Not cheap. The idea of cutting that tuition bill in half was quite appealing, so I kept my eyes open for potential nursing jobs at this particular hospital.

After graduating from Capital University, I worked in a cardiac stepdown unit, followed by a stint in labor and delivery. I eventually found a job opening in the operating room (OR) at this particular hospital. I had always loved the idea of possibly working in surgery. I thought this could be a great career opportunity if the hospital would be willing to train me in a new specialty of nursing. Long story short, I applied for the position, got an interview, and was offered the job.

This OR position actually turned out to be even better than I had expected. I was part of a great group of experienced nurses whom I could learn from. Plus, it was fascinating to see the different types of surgeries that were performed each day. I had a front row seat to watch the surgeons remove tumors, put bones back together, or transplant a kidney. Kevin has told me how he will sometimes remind his team at work during stressful moments that they are "not saving lives." However, in my new job, we were *literally* saving lives!

July 24, 2007

This was the day when my life changed forever. This day began like any other day in the operating room. My role was to be a floating nurse, which meant covering for the other nurses during their breaks, prepping rooms for surgery, and being on call for potential emergency trauma cases. That afternoon, while a scrub tech and I were getting a room ready, I was asked to cover for a neuro nurse in surgery so she could take a quick bathroom break. This seemed like great timing because I needed to go into that operating room at some point to get a piece of equipment for the other room we were prepping.

After entering that room, I let the nurse know I was there to give her a break. She then gave me a quick update on what was happening before leaving. I looked over the charting before getting in place to observe the surgery currently taking place. While standing there, I saw the piece of equipment needed for the other OR room called a Midas Rex. It was an electrical piece of equipment sitting on a metal tower with several shelves. Each shelf on this tower had a piece of electrical equipment plugged into the attached power strip. At the bottom of this tower were metal sleds, which look exactly like they sound. The sleds are used during surgery to tuck a patient's arm against their side so the surgeon can freely walk around the table without bumping into them.

The piece of equipment I needed was not going to be used during the craniotomy (brain surgery) they were performing. Before the nurse came back, I started to assess the tower and locate where the Midas Rex device was plugged into. Since there were multiple things on this tower plugged into the same power strip, all the cords and cables were tangled. I decided to move the gray cord that was plugged in the top slot of the power strip, and when I did, everything changed.

Instantly, an electrical current went up my right index finger, my right arm, and then throughout my entire body. I heard several loud pops and then sparks flew inside this operating room. I immediately jerked my arm back and started shaking it really hard. I remember the room froze and all eyes were staring at me. Everyone was kind of nervous, hoping I was okay. Then the nurse I had replaced came walking back into the room from her break as I continued to shake my right arm in pain. Another neuro scrub tech helped me walk out of the OR and asked if I was "okay." I told her, "Yes, but my head feels staticky." She walked with me back to the other OR room to finish preparing it for surgery.

As I was trying to prep the room, the man who handled our neuro-surgery equipment came into the OR. He had just seen the room where the accident happened and wanted to check on me. He said, "Stephanie you need to see the OR. I mean, look at these sleds!" He was carrying the two metal sleds that had been stacked on top of each other at the bottom of that metal tower. There were two holes blasted through each of them. So my scrub tech and I quickly followed him back to the scene of the accident. The surgery was over and he had been assessing the damage to the room and equipment. I was astonished by what I saw.

There was ash residue all over the wall, which was a good ten feet away from where I had been standing. The power strip was completely black from getting fried by the electrical surge.

Angels were protecting me.

When I walked back to the other room, I received a phone call from one of the nursing supervisors. She was a close friend of mine and wanted to know if I was okay. I said "Jami, it's just my head. My head is feeling really weird right now, but I'll be fine." Then a manager came into the room to check on me. As she got to within a few feet of me, she said, "Stephanie, I can smell you. You smell like you have been singed!" Yet there were no burn marks on me at all.

She immediately sent me down to visit employee health. At employee health, they took my vitals and noticed my blood pressure had dropped significantly. They did an EKG, which showed my heart was in an irregular rhythm, but then told me I should be fine and could return to work tomorrow.

When I got back to my floor, I told the in-charge nurse about my experience with employee health and she would not let me drive home. Instead, she arranged for someone who lived close to our neighborhood to drive me home.

Wow…what a day.

Twelve Years Later…and I Am Getting Mad AGAIN
(Written by Kevin Mason)

I remember getting a phone call from Stephanie saying she had been injured at work. Of course, she downplayed it and told me she was fine and didn't need me to rush home. I later found out it was a miracle she had not been killed instantly.

I feel so blessed and am so thankful I did not lose my wife that day in the OR. However, it is now twelve years later…and I am getting mad AGAIN. It's kind of hard not to after reading what Stephanie wrote and I start to feel and relive all those emotions again.

I'm sorry folks, but this is the kind of crap that gets me fired up! How is it even possible to have this type of incompetence at an employee health department? Why even have an employee health department if you are just going to send people back to work regardless of what their symptoms are? Does this department just take your vitals to check the box that they actually did something?

Who, in this employee health department, was trying to help my wife? If there was ever a time when an employee should probably get looked at further, THIS WOULD HAVE BEEN THAT TIME!

People could smell my wife after literally getting fried from the electrical shock. Her blood pressure was low. Her heart had an irregular rhythm. How could someone, who is supposed to be educated and compassionate toward others, tell my wife to go ahead and return back to work? How could someone approve her to go back upstairs and take care of patients, when she couldn't even think clearly at that moment?

Are you freaking kidding me!

I asked Stephanie if there was an actual real-life nurse working in employee health that day or if it could have been one of the cleaning ladies (no offense to cleaning ladies). She told me a DOCTOR had sent her back to work!

ARE YOU FREAKING KIDDING ME!

Thank God for angels protecting my wife that day. Thank God, there were some great nurses Stephanie worked with who checked on my wife and helped her get home safely. How would you feel if this happened to your spouse? Or your mother? Or one of your children?

Would you be okay if their employer just sent them back to work and acted as if nothing happened? Unless you don't like your family, I am guessing you would probably have similar feelings.

You Need to Come Back to the Hospital

After getting home, I tried calling my husband, but he was in a meeting so I had to leave him a voicemail. Since I did not know how serious this was yet, I did not want to call my parents to avoid causing them to worry. After about an hour at home, Jami, who is such a great person and friend, called to check on me. She told me some of the surgeons had been talking and were baffled this had happened. They were even more surprised when they found out I had been sent home. They said I should have spent the night at the hospital and been placed on a Holter monitor for my heart. With the amount of voltage I received, they were concerned my heart could stop at any minute.

Jami tried to convince me to come back to the hospital to get checked out again. I told her that Kevin was not home yet and the last thing I wanted to do was go to the ER, sit for hours, and then be sent home again.

In hindsight, I probably should have called for the squad or someone to come get me. This was a little more serious than I had originally thought, but I really just wanted to go to bed.

I got off the phone and did the only thing I knew to do. I prayed and I prayed *hard.* I prayed that God would protect my heart and keep it pumping. I prayed that God would keep me safe…and allow me to wake up in the morning. Kevin finally got my voicemail and called me back. I explained the situation and told him I was going to bed. I remember asking him to check on me when he got home to make sure I was still breathing. It was an odd request to have to give your spouse.

My Head Hurts

The next day, my alarm woke me up. I just laid in bed and looked at the ceiling thinking, *My heart didn't stop, I am not in any pain, I must be fine.* Unfortunately, I was wrong. This would be the first of many painful days ahead for me.

I stood up to get out of bed and my head hurt so bad I had to immediately lie back down. The pain focused right around my forehead where I had told my scrub tech my head felt "staticky." I called the OR and explained how I was feeling and they advised me to stay home. Later that day, I noticed my stomach started to quiver intermittently. As I laid in bed, I watched my stomach shaking. Then I started to cramp really bad. I was nervous about the impact this accident was having on my body. This was starting to get scary.

For the next five days, I was either on the couch or in bed. I could not do anything when standing up because the pressure I felt in my head was too overwhelming. I needed to be lying down horizontally to be even a little bit comfortable. I would try to watch some TV, but the slightest thing, like fast-forwarding, would intensify my headaches.

The following week, I was still not feeling right but tried to go back to work since I had taken an entire week off. When I got to work, I was honest with the nursing manager regarding how I was feeling and she immediately sent me to see employee health (again). The doctor down there was surprised to hear of all the side effects I had been experiencing and referred me to see another doctor at the hospital. Dr. Schaub became my new point of contact for all matters related to the electrical injury. Dr. Schaub, who is now retired, was absolutely amazing. He was so caring, compassionate, and kind to me. He was a doctor who would take all the time needed to listen to me and then do everything in his power to help. After meeting with him the first time, he ordered a CT scan and some neurological testing for me. The results showed the frontal and parietal lobe of my brain, for lack of a better word, had been "fried."

More Symptoms

As time went on, new symptoms would arise. I started having problems with short-term memory loss, cognitive thinking, and my speech. I also began to experience anxiety, mild depression, and hallucinations.

The hallucinations I started having would be completely random as they would pop up at different times and I would have no idea what may have caused them. For example, one day, I decided to empty the trash can in our kitchen. As I stepped on the pedal to open the lid, thousands of gnats flew out of the trash. I started screaming and swatting them away until they, all of a sudden, disappeared.

Another time, I was in the basement watching TV when I saw a mammoth spider crawling across the floor. I grabbed something to kill it, and then again, it was gone.

Another day, I remember coming down the stairs and seeing a huge hot pink stain on our eggplant-colored couch. I immediately yelled for Kevin to ask him how this happened, to which he had no idea what I was talking about. I just went to the kitchen and said to myself, "It's no big deal, don't get mad! I will just flip the cushion over and no one will ever know." When I went back to flip the cushion over, the hot pink stain was gone.

It was scary because these moments seemed so incredibly real to me.

Don't Leave Me

I had always been a person who loved to go out with Kevin or to socialize with friends. Now, I didn't even want to leave the house. Having a conversation with anyone became challenging, stressful, and embarrassing. I would constantly get my words mixed up or stop mid-sentence and not be able to think of the word I was trying to articulate. For example, I would mistakenly ask Kevin to shut the door but actually meant the window. My words were constantly getting mixed up.

The issues I started having with short-term memory loss made things particularly challenging for those closest to me. One night while eating dinner with Kevin, I asked him how his day went, and he looked at me as if he were annoyed. I snapped at him to ask what his problem was! He said I had already asked him "how did your day go" three times since we started eating dinner. I had no idea I was doing this. Just trying to have a normal, relaxing dinner with my husband became difficult.

If Kevin and I were to go out to dinner with another couple, I would not let him leave to go to the bathroom, no matter if they were our closest friends. I was so afraid that I was going to say something stupid or have trouble speaking to someone without him there.

During one particular dinner, my poor husband probably drank about six glasses of iced tea and I wouldn't let him leave the table. Not sure why he was so thirsty that night, but he was like a camel seeing water for the first time. I knew he was probably hurting, but whenever he would try to get up to head for the restroom, I would dig my fingers into his knee. I was so nervous for him to leave me alone I would have tears in my eyes. It was an awful feeling.

(Kevin said you should have some sympathy for him too since holding it for the entire meal is an awful feeling as well.)

I also hated to leave the house by myself for a doctor's appointment because I was scared that I would not be able to remember where I parked. (Remember, kids, this was during a time when there were no iPhones for me to take a picture of where I had parked or an app to track where my car was. I imagine this is probably blowing some of your millennial minds right now.)

I Felt Helpless
(Written by Kevin Mason)

One of the weird things about Stephanie's brain injury was that you could not tell anything was wrong by just looking at her. She was as gorgeous as ever. But if you talked to her for a few minutes, you would be able to tell something was off.

She would constantly get her words mixed up. An example might be her telling me to put something in the microwave, but she actually meant the fridge. It was close, but not the same.

There were some days that felt like the movie *50 First Dates* because of her short-term memory issues. One time at church, we were talking to Mike out in the hallway. Stephanie asked him how work was going. He answered.

Thirty seconds later…"Hey Mike, how is your new job going?" He politely answered her again.

Then *another* thirty seconds later…"Mike, didn't you get a new job?"

It's funny now…but it was not funny back then. It's not funny when you live this on a daily basis.

One thing that really proved to me that my wife had some type of brain injury was when she had me do some math exercises with her. I would ask her simple multiplication, addition, and subtraction problems that an elementary kid would know.

What is 2+2? "Four!"

What is 4+4? "Eight!"

What is 2×4? "Six!"

Stephanie had a tough time flipping the switch to a different topic. Not only that, but if she were to really focus on having a conversation with someone or try to read a book, it would lead to her having some major migraine-type headaches. But they weren't migraines. You couldn't just give her medication like you would for a migraine because her pain was from her brain injury. She tried so many medications over those three to four years just to try to live somewhat of a normal life. Most of the time, she was in bed by the time I got home. If we went out on the weekend to spend time with family or friends, the next day, she would be completely wiped out.

There were times when the medication she was given wouldn't even touch the pain she was in. There were three instances when I had to rush my wife to the emergency room in the middle of the night. The pain in her head would become too unbearable to deal with. That says a lot because Stephanie has an incredibly high tolerance for pain. Each time this happened, the ER would give her some type of a concoction to take the pain away. However, this concoction of medicine would also put her to sleep for the next sixteen to twenty hours. It would completely knock her out.

As a husband, I felt helpless. Seeing my wife in constant pain and lying in a hospital bed was gut-wrenching for me. She didn't sign up for this. She had worked so hard to get through school, pass her board exam, and start her nursing career. Now this?

What could I do to help? I didn't know what to do. Her various doctors didn't even know what to do.

After two and a half years of living this, I decided to write an email to our family and a few close friends. Here is that email from January 30, 2010.

Friends and family,

I am asking all of you to be in prayer and agreement with me in regards to Stephanie's healing. In July, it will be three full years since she was electrocuted. We need a miracle. Again, it looks like all doors are closing…so we need God to smash open a window or door or roof for my wife. A doctor a few weeks ago told Steph that he was shocked that she was still here based on the amount of nerve damage she has suffered. I see the facts…but I am refusing to accept them. I reject the doctors' report. I am going to believe the report of the Lord. I believe this is the year we see my wife FULLY healed and recover everything that has been lost and stolen from her. I am claiming her healing. Please, please, please…I need each one of you to be in agreement with me in prayer each and every day this year for my wife. We are claiming her healing, we are claiming her energy to be restored, we are claiming her hallucinations to cease, we are claiming her memory to be restored, we are claiming all brain and nerve damage to be repaired, and we are claiming our future children.

I hope you can sense my level of sincerity and the significance of my request. Thank you for being so supportive of both Stephanie and me. We love you all and appreciate your prayers.

Sincerely,

Kevin

My New Occupation

By the summer of 2010, it had been three long, tough years and I was constantly going to doctors' appointments. This became my new occupation. I felt sad, alone, and frustrated. New symptoms continued to pop up and I was nowhere near ready to go back to work.

For the most part, the doctors I met with were consistently perplexed and would tell me how challenging it was for them to treat me. They said the brain is so complex and incredibly difficult to treat, that it could take years for my brain to heal. That is IF it were to ever heal.

I asked if they thought I would be able to have children, and one of my doctors said, "Oh, don't even think about having children!" I was devastated. It felt like my heart had just been ripped out of my chest. What do you mean "don't even think about having children"? I wanted to someday have a family. My husband wanted to have a family. I remember Kevin and I even playfully discussing our future children when we were dating. This was something we had been looking forward to. We were now going on six years of marriage, which was well past the time we had initially planned to "start having kids".

This comment by my doctor really got to me. Mentally, I felt defeated. I wanted answers. So I contacted the National Institute of Health (NIH), which does a lot of health-related research. After sharing my story, they responded with an apology stating they would not be able to help me either. They said the patients who experienced what I had were typically from lighting strikes and did not survive.

No More Doctor's Appointments for Me
(*Written by Kevin Mason*)

After three years of doctors' appointments, we were not making much progress…if any. Every doctor we met with seemed clueless with how to treat Stephanie or even help her. This led to me eventually getting a little frustrated. Then this little frustration led to me eventually embarrassing my wife. While at one particular appointment:

Doctor:	"Now, Stephanie, please remind me which medications you have been on. Have you tried *blah blah blah*?"
Stephanie:	"Yes."
Doctor:	"What about *blah blah blah*?"
Stephanie:	"Yes."
Doctor:	"Great. What about *blah blah blah*?"
Stephanie:	"No."
Doctor:	"Okay, then why don't we try that one this time?"
Me:	"I'm sorry, doctor, but are you just *guessing* here?! It seems to me like you are guessing! How is what you are doing any different than me looking on the Internet and playing *'Pick a Lucky Winner'* with her medication? *Did this one work…nope. How about this one…nope. Okay, let's try this one!*"
Stephanie:	(Shaking her head in disbelief.)

The doctor then politely gave me a dissertation on how medication is broken into different phases of *blah blah blah*.

This was the final appointment I ever went to with Stephanie related to her electrical injury. For some reason, she no longer ~~wanted~~ needed me to attend.

Am I Pregnant?

In July 2010, my period stopped. Initially, I was ECSTATIC! I thought this meant I was pregnant. I took a pregnancy test and it was negative. I kept looking at the stick and waiting and waiting. How could it be negative? I was confused.

By September, with still no period and more negative pregnancy tests, it finally hit me. This was another symptom caused by my electrical injury. I cried. Not just a sad cry. This was uncontrollable crying. I began yelling and then questioning God. My life had turned into so much sadness. I was constantly in pain and thinking about the woman I used to be.

I then realized I needed to get my obstetrician (OB) involved with my string of doctors to figure out why my period had disappeared. When I saw my OB, she didn't have many answers for me either. By November of that year, I still had not had a period, so my OB prescribed some medicine that would help start my period again.

However, I soon found out you can actually get pregnant supernaturally without having a period.

You can't tell by looking at Stephanie, but
she was actually electrocuted.

You can't tell by looking at my haircut,
but I was NOT electrocuted.

CHAPTER 5

BABY FAITH

* Unless noted otherwise, this chapter was written by Stephanie Mason.

My Husband's Pain

I didn't realize how much my health had impacted my husband. When Kevin gets focused on something, he is a machine. He will grind through whatever when life gets tough—deadlines at work, getting his MBA, or writing this book. He just keeps going. However, there came a moment when I saw my strong husbands' emotional wall come down. I didn't know it, but he was hurting too.

A few weeks before Kevin finished his MBA program, we were in church, and at the end of the service, there was an opportunity for people to go down front for prayer. Kevin left his seat and walked down to receive prayer. I was curious to know what he wanted prayer for but stayed in my seat and let him go alone. As the service ended, I hung out by our seat and started talking with some of our best friends, Paul and Michelle. After a brief moment, Paul walked up front and started to pray for Kevin alongside someone else. After continuing to talk to Michelle a few more minutes, I looked up and saw my husband hugging Paul and sobbing. I had never seen him anywhere near this emotional before. Never. My heart broke.

As he walked back to where we had been sitting, he looked like a broken man. He was emotionally crushed, so much, in fact, that he couldn't even talk.

I went ahead and drove us back home in his car as he tried to gain his composure. In the car, he still could not speak. Whenever he would attempt to say something to me, he would immediately break down in tears again.

Later that day, he was finally able to share with me what had been bothering him. He said, during church that morning, he was thinking about children. Our future children. The dream of having a family with me had been crushed by what my doctors were telling us. Unless God were to intervene, we were not going to have any children. Starting a family looked nearly impossible and he was overcome with grief at this reality.

At that moment, it hit me how much my husband had been struggling with my health situation. I felt like I was the only one who had been suffering. Then seeing the impact my condition was having on Kevin broke my heart.

Vacation

That December, Kevin graduated with his MBA from Ohio University and we planned a vacation to get away and celebrate. As with any MBA program, my husband was consumed with group projects, case studies, papers to write, and a ton of reading for about two full years. Of course, this was on top of his full-time job at JPMorgan Chase and dealing with all of my health issues. We needed to get away, just the two of us. We needed some time away to just focus on each other.

During our vacation at Clearwater Beach, Florida, I read a book called *Supernatural Childbirth* by Jackie Mize. This book was full of encouraging stories of women getting pregnant and delivering healthy babies when they were told by doctors it would never happen. I clung to each chapter as if it were my lifeline. I quickly read through the book and then read it again. If this could happen to them, why not to me?

Then I read Pastor Gary Keesee's *Faith Hunt* book. It talked about when you pray, believe you receive it by faith. It talked about being fully persuaded that you knew...that you knew...that you knew that you had whatever you were believing God for. I remember sitting in a chair by the pool as I read these books. I started praying, and when I was done, I believed I was pregnant. It was so strange. I had never felt like this before, but I knew that I was pregnant. Nothing was going to change my mind.

When we went up to our room to get ready for dinner, I told Kevin that I believed I was pregnant. He just looked at me, not sure if I was hallucinating again. I said, "I know this sounds crazy, but I am speaking by faith that I am pregnant. Let's trust God for a baby." The rest of that trip, we talked about baby names and how we could tell our parents. We even went shopping for baby clothes. We had the best time.

On our last night of vacation, I started to suffer from another of those debilitating headaches. That night felt like one of the longest nights of my life. I was in so much pain. Kevin wanted to take me to the hospital, but I did not want to go. Nor did I want to take any type of shot or pill because we were believing I was pregnant. I was not going to take anything for these headaches and risk hurting our baby.

Back Home

I suffered all night, then all morning on the plane, and then all the way home from the airport. I could not get any relief. Kevin pleaded with me to give myself a shot because of the amount of pain I was in (my doctor had prescribed a morphine injection if the headaches got really bad). Instead, I took a pregnancy test which read "negative." I was shocked. I did not understand how it could possibly be negative.

I knew without a doubt I was pregnant, but the test said otherwise. So I went ahead and gave myself the shot to alleviate some of the pain

I was in. Before I did, I prayed. I remember telling God I still believed I was pregnant, even though the test said otherwise. I asked God to protect our baby from this medicine. Then I fell asleep.

A week or two later, I reached out to my OB to have a conversation about what to do next. She wanted me to try the medicine again that would supposedly help me start my period. Before starting back on this medication, I had to take another pregnancy test. I woke up early the next morning and decided to take the test before Kevin got up. I took the test and let it sit for about five minutes. I finally went back to the bathroom to check the test and it was POSITIVE! Wait what, no way, OMG, OMG, OMG, EEEEEKKK!

It was *positive*!

The next day, I called my OB's office again to tell them I had taken another pregnancy test and this time it was showing positive. The woman asked me when my last period was (standard question), which I then answered with "July." The phone went silent. It was January.

I don't think she knew what to say. She finally said they would need to see me to determine how far along I was. I could not wait for that OB appointment! I then called Kevin at work and asked him to pick up another pregnancy test for me on his way home. However, I wanted one of those tests that actually said the word "PREGNANT" on it. As soon as he got home, I ran upstairs to take the test before we had dinner. This was a moment when the devil would try to steal my joy. The test read "NOT PREGNANT"! I now held a negative test alongside the positive test I had taken the other day. I went from being excited to being con-fused. What was going on?

The rest of the night, all I could think about was that negative test. I finally told Kevin that I wanted to take another test to try to ease my concerns. I went to the bathroom and took that one. Same heartbroken result. It showed "NOT PREGNANT."

My husband looked at me and said, "Stephanie, we know you are pregnant. We prayed, believed, and we call it done. Those tests are wrong." I clung to those words.

Mark 11:24 (NIV) says, *"whatever you ask for in prayer, believe you have received it, and it will be yours."* I continued to believe I was pregnant. This negative test was not going to distract me from God's blessing.

A few days later, it was finally time for my doctor's appointment. I had my positive pregnancy test wrapped in toilet paper inside my purse, just in case I needed to show my doctor I had a positive test. Before my OB came in the room to do the ultrasound, I told Kevin to "pray our baby looks like a peanut instead of a pea." If it looked like a peanut, it would mean we were further along. Then my doctor walked in and it was time for the ultrasound.

The Ultrasound

My heart felt like it was beating out of my chest. I was so nervous and yet so excited. As soon as she placed the ultrasound probe inside me, we saw the most beautiful sight EVER!

We saw our baby!

Our baby had arms and legs and was moving everywhere. It was official…I was pregnant!

Not only that, but I was over ten weeks pregnant. I was almost through the first trimester! The due date they gave me was September 20, 2011, which meant we had been in Florida when I had conceived the baby. That also meant when I told Kevin I believed I was pregnant, I was pregnant. The *multiple* pregnancy tests that showed "negative" were all wrong.

During my pregnancy, all the symptoms and side effects from the electrocution were supernaturally gone. Not only had I miraculously gotten pregnant, but I was also miraculously healed from my electrocution. In Florida, I knew I was pregnant. Now, I knew I was healed.

Let's Go to Target!
(*Written by Kevin Mason*)

It's been a minute since I ~~confessed~~ mentioned a story about me doing something silly. We have been sharing a lot of serious stuff, so hopefully, this story will make you laugh…or at least crack a smile.

As you know by now, my entire professional career has been in accounting and finance. So it should come as no surprise when I tell you that I am a big numbers guy. Being a numbers guy can, apparently, go to the extreme in my personal life as well. When Stephanie was about thirty-eight weeks pregnant with Emme, I was secretly praying for our firstborn child to have a birthday of 9/10/11. I thought that would be really cool and really easy for me to remember. However, I did NOT want Emme to have a birthday one date later on 9/11. That would just feel unpatriotic!

As a soon-to-be rookie dad, who did not know crap about how the labor and delivery process actually worked, I did my best to come up with a plan for Stephanie to go into labor the night of 9/9/11. I thought starting my plan a day earlier would give my wife plenty of time for the labor process and result in our baby being born on 9/10/11. So stupid!

During the afternoon of 9/9/11, I somehow convinced my very pregnant and very uncomfortable wife that we should attempt to naturally induce her labor. In my selfish, overly excited, "can't wait to be a dad" mindset, we were going to have a baby…like right now! Instead of doing what you probably think I wanted to do, we decided to go to Target and walk around. Right before leaving for the store, my sister-in-law, Katie, came over to the house to check on Stephanie. Needless to say, we brought her with us on a trip to Target that she will *never* forget! If you ever meet Katie, you should ask her about that one time she went to Target with us, and I guarantee she will immediately bust out laughing.

Not long after we got to the store, I had to remind Stephanie and Katie to NOT stop every dang time they saw a cute little baby item. Don't get distracted, ladies! This was a business trip, not a shopping trip!

After about thirty minutes of us walking laps around the store, nothing was happening. So I felt the need to crank this workout up a notch if we wanted to start seeing some results. I went over to the sporting goods aisle and grabbed a couple of pink ten-pound dumbbells and handed them to my wife to walk with. I mistakenly thought that would do the trick. (What on God's green earth was I thinking? Why did I think I needed my wife to do some type of Beachbody workout to pop out a baby?)

My very pregnant and very uncomfortable wife was now walking around Target carrying pink dumbbells while her personal trainer (me) encouraged her to keep going. "Steph, you can do this! You're a warrior! You're a BEAST! You will forget ALL about this pain as soon as you see that baby!"

Easy for me to say. Unfortunately, those dumbbells did absolutely nothing! They just made my wife more tired. I can only imagine how silly we must have looked with Stephanie walking slower and slower around the store...and me getting louder and louder with my motivational words.

After about an hour of this complete nonsense, we decided to end my make-it-up-as-you-go workout due to Stephanie being exhausted and having a lot of back pain. That meant we would have to move onto Phase 2 of my "Project 9–10–11." Desperate times call for desperate measures!

Phase 2 was not good (not that Phase 1 was either). Unfortunately for Stephanie, Phase 2 was derived from the old wives' tales we heard from our mothers about inducing labor. They had both talked about drinking castor oil when they were pregnant to activate the labor process. Just like with twilight sleep, if it worked for them, it could work for us!

(For you, millennials out there, who have never heard of "twilight sleep," look it up. It will blow your mind how stupid humans used to be.)

We bought some castor oil and some orange juice. As soon as we got home, Stephanie grabbed a small glass and poured about three ounces of OJ and then about three ounces of oil. It did not mix...AT ALL. The oil literally just sat on top of the orange juice in the glass, like something straight out of a science experiment. Remember the saying, "oil and water don't mix"? Well, we can add another saying called, "oil and orange juice don't mix either"!

At that moment, I thought, maybe this wasn't such a good idea. Phase 2 of my plan looked absolutely disgusting. Regrettably, my wife was fully committed to my dumb "Project 9–10–11" and rapidly stirred this concoction and chugged it. (I never thought of this until just now, but my wife has a REAL talent with chugging drinks—i.e., flaming shot in Mexico.)

Sadly, we got the same non-result as Phase 1 of my plan...but with a few side effects this time. (I kind of feel bad using the word "we" here since none of this plan negatively affected me.) Phase 1 made my wife exhausted and her back hurt. Phase 2 made my wife sick.

> I probably should have Googled what happens when you drink castor oil BEFORE "we" started Phase 2.
>
> Google *question*: "Can you drink castor oil?"
> Google *answer*: "Because *castor oil* works so fast, it's not a good idea to take it before bedtime, as *you* might do with other laxatives."[1]

Oops. Sorry about that, Stephanie! Thanks for being such a trooper with Project 9–10–11! I just shake my head at these dumb moments. Sadly, this story is just the tip of the iceberg when it comes to being married to me.

Too Excited
(Written by Kevin Mason)

I cannot even begin to tell you how excited I was to become a dad. Oh my goodness! I was so amped up and excited I had a tough time getting to sleep each night. I would just toss and turn in bed, thinking about what it was going to be like to hold our baby girl for the first time. I actually started sleeping on the ottoman chair in our bedroom to keep from waking Stephanie up at night. I couldn't wait to meet her!

---

[1] Stephanie Watson, *How to Use Castor Oil to Relieve Constipation*, December 14, 2018, https://www.healthline.com/health/digestive-health/castor-oil-for-constipation (accessed September 26, 2019).

During the final month of Stephanie's pregnancy, I told her I would be treating my cell phone at work as if it were the "bat phone." I would keep my phone on me at all times. If she needed something insignificant, I asked her to just text me her request or text me to call her. Otherwise, if she called while I was at work, I was going to drop whatever I was doing and drive home like a scene straight out of *Mad Max*.

After having this conversation with my wife, it was maybe a week later when Stephanie called the bat phone while I was at work. I was in the middle of a meeting with about ten other people in one of the conference rooms at JPMorgan Chase. When I saw her phone number pop up on my phone, it was like the fire alarm had gone off in the building. I immediately jumped up out of my chair and walked out of the conference room. As soon as I got out in the hallway…

Me:	"HELLO STEPH?! IS IT TIME? I AM ON MY WAY RIGHT NOW!"
Stephanie:	"OH…that's right! I forgot! I am not supposed to call you anymore unless it's an emergency. I am so sorry."
Me:	(Now trying to catch my breath.) "So it's NOT go time yet?"
Stephanie:	"Oh no. I just wanted to see if you could bring some Chipotle home after work tonight."

You can imagine my embarrassment when I had to walk back into that conference room. "Sorry about that, folks. False alarm. My bad!"

Emme Mason
(Written by Kevin Mason)

Two days after the original due date, it was finally go time! Stephanie woke me up in the ottoman chair to tell me it was time. It was around 5:00 a.m. and I instantly jumped out of that chair to get ready. Her water hadn't broke, but she was in A LOT of pain! If this wasn't go time, we were in trouble.

At 1:15 p.m., we got to meet Emme Marie Faith Mason for the very first time. What an experience that was! Seeing the delivery process for the first time was mind-blowing. Emme was the most beautiful, cuddly little girl in the whole world! She was born on September 22nd and weighed eight pounds and two ounces and was twenty inches long. She was also the very first grandchild on Stephanie's side of the family. Such an incredible and special moment.

Emme was perfectly healthy in every way. The medication that Stephanie had taken for her headaches when we got back from Florida had zero impact on our baby girl. Stephanie carried her full term AND was able to nurse her for an entire year. Thank you, God!

Emme Marie Faith was named after her aunt, Katie Marie Schnetzer. We also included the name "Faith" as part of her middle name because of the faith that was required of us to have her. As you will read, Emme was the first of our three miracle babies.

This morning at breakfast, Emme asked if I was done writing her chapter yet. I told her I planned to finish it by the end of that day. She said, "Good. Please let everyone know I have been the best child to raise of the three of us...and how much I love unicorns!"

I thought it was ironic she mentioned loving unicorns. She truly is just like her mother.

CHAPTER 6

Stephanie's Brain Tumor

Introduction

Only two short years later, we would face our next Goliath. Becoming parents had been even better than we ever imagined and we wanted to have another baby. Not long after Emme's first birthday, we decided to start trying for a second child. By Emme's second birthday, we were still trying for a second child. I just assumed this was part of the normal, stressful, and frustrating process of trying to conceive a baby. I didn't know what "normal" was since Stephanie had miraculously conceived Emme without even having a cycle. I honestly didn't realize that trying for over a year was atypical.

Toward the end of that winter, and after a frustrating eighteen to twenty months of "trying," Stephanie mentioned wanting to get checked out by her doctor. We did not think there was anything wrong because she actually felt better than she had in years. However, it wouldn't hurt to set up an appointment to confirm that nothing was wrong.

Guess what? There absolutely was something wrong.

The Brain Tumor
(Written by Stephanie Mason)

I was sitting in my OB's office, speaking with her about our struggle with conceiving another baby. I still did not have my period, but that really did not matter to me since I did not have one when I conceived Emme. At this point, I felt completely healed from the electrocution. The only physical issues bothering me was my battle with losing the weight from Emme, along with lactating, even though I had quit nursing over a year ago. After talking with my OB, she took some blood work. A few days later, I received a phone call stating my hormones were a little "off," and they would be referring me to an endocrinologist. I honestly did not think anything would come from this referral. However, if an endocrinologist was going to help me figure out why I could not get pregnant, then I was going to go.

About a month later, I was at our rental property to meet someone who wanted to take a look at it. I wanted to make sure I got there early to ensure everything would look nice. As I was cleaning things up in the kitchen, my phone rang and it was a number I did not recognize. Typically, I will let these go to my voicemail, but for some reason, I answered this one.

Stephanie:	"Hello."
Doctor:	"Hi Stephanie, this is Dr. So-and-So."
Stephanie:	"Hello. I went this morning to have my MRI."
Doctor:	"I know. That is why I am calling. We found a mass pressing against your pituitary gland." (Silence)
Stephanie:	"Okay…what does this mean? A mass…as in you found a brain tumor?"
Doctor:	"Yes. I want you to see a neurosurgeon. I will have my office set everything up and then get in contact with you."

Stephanie: "Is it cancerous?"

Doctor: "It does not appear to be, but we cannot be 100% certain at this point."

Wow. That was not the conversation I was expecting to have.

As soon as I hung up the phone, I prayed, "God, please help me get through this." As soon as those words came out of my mouth, this unexplainable peace just washed over me. At that moment, I knew everything was going to be okay. Then the doorbell rang and I had to put on my best poker face to the woman on the other side of the front door.

The remainder of the day, I kept replaying the doctor's words in my head, *"We found a mass."* I was completely shocked.

Later that night, after I put Emme to bed, it was time to tell my husband. I was doing so good until the moment I started telling Kevin. That was when the tears started flowing. My husband prayed with me, and I kept trying to remember that peace that had come over me at our rental property. Everything was going to be okay.

We decided to get a second opinion from another endocrinologist, but that resulted in the same diagnosis. We also had a meeting with a neuro-opthamologist who spent a couple of hours going through vision screenings to see if my vision had been compromised in any way. At the end of all the exams, the neuro-opthamologist was in complete shock. He said, "With the size of your tumor and location, I cannot believe your vision has not been affected."

The tumor was pressing against my optic nerve. He continued to say, if it were to get any bigger, my vision could be affected and lost permanently.

I went back to my neurosurgeon and he recommended having surgery promptly. Of course, my primary concern was actually on having more children. They said it *could* be possible for me to conceive, but it might take months, if not years, for that to happen.

He then started to schedule my surgery, which made me freeze. Remember, I had previously worked as a neuro nurse. I knew which operating rooms they performed these surgeries in. He then said the exact operating room number where I had been electrocuted seven years earlier. That was NOT going to work.

I proceeded to tell him what had happened to me in that operating room. His mouth dropped and he said, "That was you?" He quickly changed the surgery to another hospital, and for that, I will forever be grateful to him (one of the many reasons I will be grateful for him).

Not. Good.

Stephanie went to her ob-gyn and had some blood work done, which came back abnormal. Her ob-gyn then referred her to an endocrinologist, who ordered some additional tests, including an MRI. When the doctor reviewed her MRI, he found a tumor on my wife's brain the size of a grape. This tumor was dangerously close to her optic nerve and apparently crushing her pituitary gland, which was now paper-thin. If you are like me and not exactly sure what that means, I learned the pituitary gland affects the process of ovulation, along with the production of hormones. (This is why Stephanie had been struggling to lose weight and still lactating.) Then the optic nerve connects your eye to your brain.

Long story short, Stephanie was going to need brain surgery to remove this tumor. My wife had gone to the doctor to figure out why she couldn't conceive a baby and walked out being told she had a brain tumor. Wow…this got serious real quick!

As you can imagine, it can be a little scary when a doctor is telling you all the issues they found out about your wife's brain. These doctors then explain all the benefits and all the risks associated with brain surgery. To be quite frank, the risks BY FAR outweigh the benefits. To prove I am not making this stuff up, here is a small excerpt from the Mayo Clinic website describing the potential risks:

"Brain surgery has the potential for risks and complications. These include bleeding, brain swelling, infection, brain damage or death. Other surgical complications may include seizures, muscle weakness, and problems with memory and thinking."[2]

Now imagine a doctor telling you this about your wife!
Not. Good.

Potential Post-surgery Issues

I also had one of Stephanie's doctors pull me aside to warn me about the potential post-surgery issues with brain surgery. He told me he didn't know what Stephanie we might see after surgery, as if we were talking about some robot experiment. He was nice about it but was essentially telling me I might have a different wife afterward. I was like, "What the freak are you talking about?" Here is what he was referring to:

"After diagnosis and treatment for a brain tumor, a person often may not be the same. Changes in behavior and thinking occur in the majority of patients at some point during their treatment. The extent of changes can vary considerably from person to person. Changes can be as subtle as mild forgetfulness or as dramatic as deep depression or abusive, violent outbursts."[3]

Oh my goodness!
Thinking about your wife having brain surgery is daunting by itself. Then thinking about what could happen to your wife *after* brain surgery is absolutely terrifying!

---

[2] Mayo Clinic Staff, *Awake brain surgery*, May 7, 2019, https://www.mayoclinic.org/tests-procedures/awake-brain-surgery/about/pac-20384913 (accessed September 27, 2019).

[3] BrainScience, *Coping With Personality & Behavioral Changes*, August 14, 2003. https://www.brainsciencefoundation.org/news/coping-personality-behavioral-changes/ (accessed September 27, 2019).

As a now worried sick husband, what could I possibly do to help my wife? I want you to seriously think about this for a second. If you were in my shoes at that moment, what would you do? I want you to actually feel a little bit of the frustration I had in that moment.

Doctors are telling me I might lose my wife.

She might have brain damage.

She might have bleeding or swelling on her brain.

You feeling my frustration yet? I'll keep going…

Doc, you are telling me if everything goes well with surgery, I could have a completely different wife than the woman I married?!

Doc, you are pulling me aside to tell me the Stephanie who wakes up after surgery might have a changed or altered personality?!

Doc, you are telling me my unicorn-like wife might experience changes in her behavior anywhere from mild forgetfulness to deep depression and abusive, violent outbursts?!

Are you freaking kidding me?!

Folks, you feeling my frustration yet? What could I possibly do? Was there anything within my control that I could do to help save my wife?

After listening to all these doctors, nothing I had ever accomplished in my life now mattered. Everything I had worked so doggone hard for was not going to help me out in this life-threatening situation. That MBA degree from Ohio University wasn't helping me out (two years of my life). That CPA license I attained in my mid-twenties wasn't doing a dang thing to save my wife (one and a half years of my life). The promotions I achieved during my career to get into management didn't matter. What about that nice, big house with the pool we bought on two acres of land in the amazing neighborhood that I worked countless hours to help renovate (another year of my life)? That house now doesn't mean blankety blank if my wife is not around to live in it with me.

What could I possibly do to help my wife? I was constantly asking myself this question. In business, you try to control the controllables. What could I control in this situation? Get her the best doctors and surgeons I could find? Already doing that. Even if we had the best team of brain specialists on the planet performing this surgery, these doctors are *practicing* medicine. They are not miracle workers. If something bad happens during the procedure, I am going to hear "I'm so sorry for your loss," while the surgeons just move onto the next surgery. Then what am I supposed to do? Just move on with life?

I felt helpless.

My Surgery
(*Written by Stephanie Mason*)

Leading up to the day of surgery, I kept praying that God would heal me instantly so I would not have to go through with surgery. However, I also knew that God had guided me to an amazing endocrinologist who then referred me to an amazing neurosurgeon. God was with me the entire time. He had been guiding me through this process, along with protecting my vision.

The night before surgery, my parents came into town to watch Emme while I would be in the hospital. That evening, I remember going upstairs to rock Emme to sleep. After surgery, I would not be able to pick up my daughter for a month due to the pressure on my brain. I had not rocked her to sleep for a long time as my normal bedtime process was putting her in the crib and having to walk away. But on this night, all I wanted to do was hug my baby. The tears came down my cheeks as I held on to Emme and prayed.

The next morning we got up early as I was the first surgery scheduled that day. As Kevin and I walked into the hospital, it was still dark. I remember Kevin wanting to take a selfie of us (see picture at the end of this chapter). My heart was pounding. I was literally walking into the hospital to have a brain tumor removed. Is this really happening?

Kevin was amazing. He tried to make me laugh and keep my attention off of what was about to happen. But when I had to say goodbye to Kevin, the tears were in my eyes. This was it. I was going back to have someone operate on my brain. I was now on a gurney as they rolled me into the operating room with lights right on me. I had done this so many times prior as the nurse. Now, the roles were reversed. Now, I was the patient. "God be with me, help me, 100…99…98…"

What Did We Do?

Throughout this process, I was just blown away by my wife's optimistic outlook and strong faith. Just like the scripture Stephanie would quote as she prepared to face this Goliath, her faith did not waver:

> *"Let us hold fast the confession of our hope without wavering, for he who promised is faithful"*.
>
> (Hebrews 10:23 ESV)

It is still astonishing to me how Stephanie was more concerned about whether or not she could have more children than her own health. Even then, she was thinking about her family instead of herself. Her questions to the doctors always seemed to end with, "Do you think I will be able to get pregnant?" The answer inevitably was always the same: "We don't know."

Getting pregnant would be the absolutely best-case scenario, BUT… it was a very low probability. We were told future children "may not be in the cards for you."

As I mentioned earlier, I had a big-time battle in my mind regarding what I could possibly do to help my wife. By the day of surgery, I realized I was going to have to relinquish all control over this situation…again.

"Do not be anxious about anything, but in every situation, by prayer and petition, with thanksgiving, present your requests to God".

(PHILIPPIANS 4:6 NIV)

In this situation, what options did we have?

1. We could live in fear, OR
2. We could live in faith and trust God...again.

"Alex, we'll take the 'live in faith and trust God' option for $600."

We had to remind ourselves that we had already seen and experienced a few miracles in our life. We could not forget what God had already brought us through: Stephanie surviving an electrocution, Stephanie getting pregnant without even having a period, Stephanie being able to carry a healthy baby full term, and all the side effects from her electrocution being completely gone.

If God could bring us through that, we knew He could bring Steph through this surgery. If God could raise Jesus and Lazarus from the dead, I was pretty sure He would be able to restore my wife's brain and body to complete health.

I was going to have to fully rely on God to heal my wife. I then prayerfully gave my wife's health to God. I prayed that God would do what only He could do. My trust was in God. Not in myself. Not in a neurosurgeon. Not in an endocrinologist. Not in a fertility doctor. Only in God.

Wow...My Wife Is One Tough Cookie

After sitting out in the waiting room for I don't know how many hours, the neurosurgeon came out to speak with me. He told me her surgery had gone really well and they had taken out an even larger tumor than anticipated. Now she would need to stay in the hospital for the next several days to recover and monitor her for any of the post-surgery side effects. Thank you, Jesus!

Stephanie came out of surgery with her nose stuffed with gauze, looking like she had just been in a fight with Apollo Creed. (Unfortunately, she did not let me take any pictures of her, so I do not have any to show you.) Until my wife went through this brain surgery, I did not fully realize my wife's incredibly high level of pain tolerance. Wow…my wife is one tough cookie!

NOT Like the Game "Operation"

Due to the location of the tumor, the doctors did not have to saw open my wife's skull for this particular surgery. Thankfully, the surgeons were able to go through Stephanie's nose to get the tumor, which was just fascinating to me.

Until just now, I thought the doctors pulled the "entire" tumor out of her nose in only one attempt. I honestly thought her surgery had been kind of like the game "Operation" where you pull the "entire" ice cream cone out of the patient's head to cure brain freeze.

A few minutes ago, I mentioned to Stephanie how amazing it was they could pull that grape-sized tumor through her nose. She then gave me that stupid look and said, "Please tell me you are kidding! PROMISE me you are kidding right now!"

I was not kidding. To me, it was like a magic trick when they pulled that thing out through her nose. She then informed me the surgeons cut the tumor into *pieces*. Then they brought those cut-up *pieces* through her nose. They did not try to take the *entire* thing out on one trip.

I am now disappointed. That is not nearly as impressive to me. That was NOT like a magic trick.

Loud As a Motorcycle

The doctors had warned me about my wife possibly being a little different after surgery, which was *kind of* true. One thing that became immediately obvious (and hilarious) to me was how my wife now had the ~~scariest~~ weirdest sneeze for about the next six weeks. She was told NOT to sneeze through her nose at all costs. The pressure from a normal sneeze could reopen the wound inside her nose. If she needed to sneeze, she had to do it with her mouth open. Her new sneeze now sounded like a Maria Sharapova tennis grunt/shriek/scream. It was a loud "AHHH HAAA!" It was loud enough to startle me from any room in the house. All pets and animals even remotely close to our home would immediately seek shelter. Her open-mouth sneeze was practically as loud as a motorcycle!

(Just kidding...but not really.)

We stayed at the hospital for the next four to five days. I slept in a chair beside Stephanie's bed at the hospital every night. I did not leave her side except to get some fresh air, go home for some clean clothes, and buy a bowling ball.

My Version of This Story

Husbands, this is one of those stories your wife *never* forgets, *never* stops bringing up, and *never* EVER lets you off the hook for. And each time she tells her version of this story, she will make it sound worse and worse. So let me get my version of this story out there.

One of my so-called bucket list items was to someday bowl a score of 200 or higher. I call this a "bucket list" item very loosely. I only bowl maybe once or twice a year. Typically, it's at a company Christmas party or some corporate event. I had actually been close to 200 a few times before, including a 184 at a corporate outing one time. However, my wife fails to appreciate how tough it is for a complete amateur to bowl a 200, especially when that amateur only bowls one to two times a year. As I researched how to bowl a 200, I found out one of the mistakes I had been making was using one of the bowling alley balls. I learned if you want to even have a fighting chance to hit the 200 mark, you cannot be using one of those beat-up bowling alley balls. Most of those balls are cracked, which makes it incredibly hard to consistently roll the ball where you want it to go.

I have also tried to stress to Stephanie (who has *never* even come close to bowling a 200 game) how stinking hard it is to go through ten frames without having an open frame (ten consecutive strikes and/or spares). The way the math works to get a 200 game is for every open frame you bowl, you will have to bowl at least two strikes in a row at some point. Not easy.

So what did I do?

I had to go buy my own bowling ball! I did a little more research and then found a good-looking bowling ball on Craigslist. This would be a birthday gift to me...from me.

On Craigslist, there was a local bowling alley in Columbus raising money for a charity. They were selling some of their bowling equipment to help raise money for this charitable cause. I thought this might be a GREAT opportunity to get my bowling ball at a GREAT price. Unfortunately, my wife and in-laws still give me crap for haggling the guy on the price of the ball. "He was selling it for charity, you cheapskate!"

I knew that, but I ALWAYS try to negotiate prices on Craigslist. It is against my religion to buy something off the website at face value. This was no exception. After negotiating with the guy, he lowered the price by $5, which I appreciated!

To make this story even worse for me, the man raising money for charity was willing to meet me beside the hospital parking garage. This probably looked like a drug deal but with a bowling ball.

By day three, I was going stir crazy inside the hospital. I had only been there for a few days, but I kind of had cabin fever. I know...I know...my wife had it MUCH, MUCH, MUCH worse than I did. Cry me a river, right?

I really wanted to get out of there for a little bit...and was just itching to try out my new birthday gift. I then recall my wife telling me that I should leave and go get some fresh air. She even recommended I go to the bowling alley to get the holes drilled in my new ball. I was like, "No... you sure? Okay, see ya!"

I pretty much sprinted out of that hospital to get to the bowling alley (which was also giving me free hole drilling as part of my charitable contribution). I then had the pro shop drill the holes on the ball several times while I tested it out. By the time I got to game #3 on the scoreboard, I was warmed up and finally had the right-size finger holes drilled.

It was at that time that I checked off another one of my ~~fictitious~~ bucket list items. Yeah, that's right…I bowled a 209 and still have the scoreboard picture to prove it! I was so happy about my accomplishment that I decided to stop at Chipotle to celebrate. Stephanie had told me to go enjoy myself, so I was going to enjoy myself!

This was a great moment for me personally. So instead of ordering my meal to go, I decided to sit outside on the patio to eat and reflect on my bowling achievement. I just sat there and thought of the endless amount of things I could accomplish with this new bowling ball. How good could I get if I bowled just one day a week after work? What if I bowled on the weekend too? Should I consider joining a league? How hard would it be to bowl a 250? This new $35 ball had just opened up a whole new world for me!

Unfortunately, when I got back to the hospital, my wife was not as impressed with my "bucket list" accomplishment as I was. I think it is fair to say she was also not in a celebratory mood like I was. The conversation went something like this:

Steph: "OMG…where have you been?!"

Me: (Excited) "Steph, you are NOT going to believe what just happened! You ready for this?
(Steph giving me a cold hard glare.)

Me: "I'll take your silence as a 'yes.' I just bowled a 209!"

Steph: (Definitely NOT excited.) "How many games did you bowl? You have been gone for like five hours!"

Me: "I only bowled three games. But I guess it did take a little bit of time for me to get the right fit with my new ball. I think I had to take it back to the pro shop about four times for the guy to redrill the holes. But it fits perfect now!"

Steph: "Then what did you do?"

Me: "Then I had to go to Chipotle to celebrate."

Steph: "Celebrate! Celebrate what?"

Me: "Okay…maybe you didn't hear me the first time. I just bowled my first 200 game EVER! Here is a picture of my score—209!"

Steph: "Did you get me anything from Chipotle?"

        (Awkward silence.)

Oops.

Looking back, I will admit…this was definitely a husband fail moment for me. I was just so excited to get out of the hospital and probably a little too excited to test out my new bowling ball. However, if you ask my wife about this story, please do NOT believe her version if she tells you:

- ❖ I bowled with those inflatable bumpers in the gutters. (My score was legit. I did not use any type of performance-enhancing equipment that day, with the exception of my new bowling ball!)
- ❖ I was gone for days.
- ❖ I was popping champagne corks at Chipotle.

I realize she was suffering in the hospital alone for a couple of hours while I was away. However, in my defense, your honor…I want to remind everyone of the fact that *SHE* WAS THE ONE WHO TOLD ME TO GET OUT OF THE HOSPITAL! That was NOT my idea! She blames me for actually doing what she told me to do! I am not a mind reader here! I was just trying to follow orders! I do not recall any restrictions being placed on "how long I should be gone" from the hospital!

Mr. and Mrs. Judge and Jury, THAT is my version of the story. I rest my case, your honor.

Fast-forward to a few big life moments we had when Stephanie decided to bring this story back up:

1. At the hospital after she delivered baby #2, "Hey Kev, you want to go bowling later tonight?"

2. While visiting me when I was staying overnight at the cancer hospital, "Darn it. I should have brought that bowling ball with me!"

3. At the hospital with baby #3, "Let me guess…you are wanting to bounce out of here to go bowling. Am I right? Or am I right!"

She thinks she is funny. (As you can probably tell, her personality did not change after surgery.)

Hindsight is 20/20. I will admit I did not handle everything perfectly in that situation. Looking back, I wish I would have paid the full amount for my new bowling ball.

Post-surgery

Remember what the doctors told us before surgery? They didn't know what kind of Stephanie we were going to get. Didn't know if she would be able to have any more children. Didn't know what her personality would be like. (Still awesome!)

About four weeks post-surgery, I was at work early for the normal Monday morning chaos that I experienced every week in the retail industry. Steph knew my Monday mornings were crazy, so she would never call or text me during this time unless it was an emergency. Around 8:30 a.m., I got a call from my wife as I was trying to finalize things for my 9:00 a.m. meeting with senior management. I nervously answered the phone, thinking this could not be good. After answering, I heard my wife crying on the other end of the line. My heart immediately sunk. I was thinking, *Oh crap! What just happened? Do I need to pack things up and rush home?*

I then heard my wife say, "Kevin, I just started my period."

A quick selfie prior to walking into the hospital.

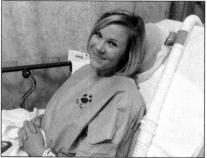

Wow... my wife looks good right before brain surgery!

Here is the visual evidence that I actually bowled a 209.
Unfortunately, my wife was not as impressed with this achievement as I was.

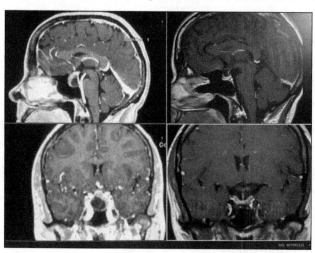

LEFT: Before surgery   **RIGHT:** After surgery

CHAPTER 7

Baby Hope

That Phone Call

Wow...what a phone call. I am glad I didn't let that one go to voicemail!

I am kidding.

I will remember that phone call forever. My wife getting her period for the first time in over four years was the first physical sign that her body was healing. I am thrilled Stephanie called, but boy, did it do a number on me that morning! I had to turn my back to my desk because I started to cry (again) when she gave me that news. Then I had about twenty-five minutes to refocus and finalize things for a big Monday morning meeting with senior management. However, that big meeting on my calendar didn't seem as important anymore. What was important was seeing my wife's health being restored.

Something Else We Did

As I mentioned in the previous chapter, there was a period of time when I was frustrated and felt thoroughly helpless regarding my wife's health. What I had to do was prayerfully give my wife and her health over to God. She was in His hands. I prayed that God would do what only He could do.

I remember something else we did when we were facing that Goliath of Stephanie's brain tumor. We kept anchoring ourselves to the word *restore*. Let me give you a quick definition of the word.

Restore

1. *(v. t.) To bring back to its former state; to bring back from a state of ruin, decay, disease, or the like; to repair; to renew; to recover.*
2. *(v. t.) To give or bring back, as that which has been lost, or taken away.*

(Source: Webster's Dictionary)

These definitions pretty much sum up our prayers. We continuously prayed that God would *restore* everything to my wife that had been lost. We spoke the Word over Stephanie and prayed everything that had been stolen from her with her health would be completely *restored*. Not only did we speak the Word, but we believed it!

We got to the point where it no longer mattered what the doctors were telling us. We understood the risks. We understood the facts. We understood the severity of the situation. *"Let God be true, and every human being a liar"* (Romans 3:4 NIV).

I heard Joel Osteen say that professionals were the ones who built the Titanic. It sank. Amateurs were the ones who built the ark. It floated. With God, all things are possible.

What was the Word of God telling us?

My Bible tells us my wife is healed (Acts 10:38).

My Bible tells us my wife is more than a conqueror (Romans 8:37).

My Bible tells us that God satisfies us with long life (Psalm 91:16).

Time to Take a Pregnancy Test

After her surgery, Stephanie was confident she was going to be pregnant. When I say "confident," I mean she knew…that she knew…that she knew…she was getting pregnant.

It was around four weeks post-surgery when Stephanie got her period again. It was around the six-week mark when we were allowed to start trying for a baby again. And it was around the eight-week mark when Stephanie started taking pregnancy tests again.

When Stephanie took that first pregnancy test, she saw a very faint line. The next day, she took another test and it showed a slightly darker line. After one week and five pregnancy tests later, my wife was finally ready to tell me what was going on.

Stephanie Mason was preggers!

I'm a Big Sister!

The moments when my wife has told me she was pregnant have been absolutely amazing. Hands down, these moments have been some of the most memorable of my life. Shocking. Emotional. Mind-boggling. All of the above.

I am thankful Stephanie was able to get this particular moment captured with her iPhone. (And I am thankful she didn't call me at work on a stressful Monday morning again to deliver the news.)

As I walked into the house one evening after work, I heard little Emme excitedly yelling something from the kitchen area and then her little footsteps running toward me. I took my shoes off, walked into the kitchen, and picked up my animated, little three-year-old. When I picked her up, she continued to enthusiastically try to tell me something while showing me her new T-shirt.

Her T-shirt said "Big Sister" on it. Then I realized she was telling me, "I'm a big sister!"

As soon as I understood Emme, I just squeezed her and hugged her tight. Then it started to get a little misty in the room. (This keeps happening to me!)

I guess it's hard *not* to get a little emotional after everything we had been through. When Stephanie saw my reaction with our daughter in my arms, she couldn't help but start to cry as well. The only one in the room *not* crying was our little preschooler. Actually, Emme seemed kind of confused because all of a sudden, her mommy and daddy were both crying. She was hugging me and hoping I was okay.

I was more than okay…because we were having another baby!

You can view this video by going to www.kevinandsteph.com.

I Get to Buy Tampons Again!
(*Written by Stephanie Mason*)

I will always remember that morning when I told Kevin I had started my period. I was shaking and crying and just saying over and over and over, "God, you are so good." I was thrilled to get my period again and everything that came with it. When the cramps started, I was actually giddy. Then came the bloating and again, I was so happy. I certainly had a different perspective than I used to about getting my period. To not have something for so long and then all of a sudden be completely restored was mind-blowing.

During my period that week, I don't think I had been that happy in a long time. I remember being proud to get to buy tampons like some thirteen-year-old girl. Then I put an app on my phone to help inform me when I would be fertile. I knew I was going to be pregnant soon.

When the time came for my next period to begin…it didn't. I could hardly wait to take a pregnancy test. As soon as I took it, I tried to wait a few minutes before looking. I prayed and told God that no matter what this test showed, I knew I was going to be pregnant again. I had faith. As I stared at the test, I didn't see anything at first. Then after *really* looking at it, I could see the faintest double line. I immediately thought, *Even though it's faint, there is still a double line!* Tears began streaming down my face. My heart was pounding.

I would take another test the next morning to see if it was stronger. Then again on days two, three, four, and five, the line got darker and darker. I was PREGNANT!

Elle McKenzie Hope Mason

Having learned a valuable lesson from my silly "Project 9–10–11" almost four years earlier, I was *not* going to try to expedite the labor process with our next child. Baby #2 was going to show up whenever she was ready. Around 9:45 p.m. EST on 6/8/15, I was lying in bed playing on my phone, while Stephanie watched *The Bachelor.*

Steph got out of bed because, like normal, she was uncomfortable and needed to stretch out a little bit. As she was leaning against the dresser, all of sudden, she grabbed her belly and said, "OH MY! I think my water just broke!"

She rushed to the bathroom and then yelled out, "Yep...my water broke! Go get Emme!"

Hearing that one sentence made me go from being tired to immediately jumping out of bed and doing some type of happy dance around the room. I am guessing it might be the same type of emotional jolt people experience when they think they've won the lottery or heard someone yell "FIRE!" inside a movie theater.

Okay...maybe not that last one. But I did go from feeling "I am tired and ready for bed" to "I am not going to sleep at all tonight because I am soooooo freaking excited!"

I ran down to Emme's room; she was already awake after hearing someone yelling from a couple of rooms away (possibly me). I grabbed our packed bags, got my girls in the car, and headed over to grandma and gramps' house.

After dropping Emme off, we drove to the hospital and Stephanie got into a room around 11:00 p.m. By 1:00 a.m., my rush of adrenaline had worn off and I was tired again. I realize I could not have been NEARLY as tired as my wife, but I was pretty darn tired. After confirming Stephanie was doing alright, I laid down on a couch in the delivery room and took a quick five-and-a-half-hour catnap.

That catnap abruptly ended around 6:30 a.m. when one of the nurses woke me up. I remember waking up to a nurse shaking my shoulder and saying, "Hey, you might want to see this."

When I came back to consciousness, I heard the nurses telling Stephanie NOT to push. She needed to wait for Dr. Turner who was on her way to the hospital. Shortly after Dr. Turner arrived, so did 'Baby Hope'. At 7:28 a.m., we met Elle McKenzie Hope Mason for the first time. We gave her the middle name of Hope after one of the verses we had been declaring during Stephanie's brain surgery:

> *"Let us hold fast the confession of our hope that it waver not; for he is faithful that promised".*
>
> (HEBREWS 10:23 ASV)

This delivery process could not have gone better. Elle was born on 6/9/15. The math was perfect for me (6+9=15), *and* I was able to take a quick nap!

Elle's Delivery
(*Written by Stephanie Mason*)

Oh, my husband! Have I mentioned how much I love him? I am so grateful Kevin did not try to convince me to go to Target again. However, it might have been because Elle was born six days early. When we got to the hospital, he could not sit down because he was so excited. I loved seeing him like this.

After I had my IV placed, monitors on, epidural placed, and the nurses exited the room, the adrenaline rush to get me to the hospital kind of wore off for Kevin. He now had to wait patiently for our little girl to arrive whenever she was ready. He told me he was going to lie down for a little bit, which actually meant we would have to wake him up for the delivery of our daughter.

I, too, was excited but very uncomfortable. Our little girl was giving me a run for my money with some insane back labor that the epidural would not touch. The nurse kept trying to adjust me but finally had to call the anesthesiologist back in to fix my epidural. Of course, my husband slept right through all of this as various people kept coming in and out of my room.

Around 6:25 a.m., I started to feel a crazy amount of pressure and thought I should get my nurse to check me again. She had just been in a few minutes earlier when I was dilated at seven or eight. When she came back, I told her I was feeling some pressure. Sure enough, Elle's head was right there! That was when the excitement picked up again and the nurse went over to wake Kevin up. I then had a crazy forty-five minutes or so. My OB was not on call that morning, but the nurses still called to let her know I was ready to deliver. I just love my OB, Dr. Paige Turner! She got out of bed and headed my way. It sure was hard to NOT push, but it was so worth it to have Dr. Turner deliver our second healthy, beautiful baby girl. When Dr. Turner put Elle on my chest, the tears just flowed. After what we had gone through over that year and a half, I was holding God's promise. And she was perfect!

It HAD to be God

For any of you reading this who may not be a believer or might be unsure if there is even a God, I want you to think about what Stephanie and I just experienced. Like this moment, there have been a lot of things I have seen and experienced that I cannot explain. Neither can our doctors.

It was priceless to see the reactions of each doctor at Stephanie's follow-up appointments. Here is what happened almost every time:

Doctor:	"Stephanie, it's been a couple of months since I last saw you. How are you feeling?"
Stephanie:	"I feel great. I am also __X__ weeks pregnant!"
Doctor:	"Wait…what?!"

These professional men and women were dumbfounded. And I loved watching every second of it. This was so rare, in fact, that Stephanie was interviewed for an article in a medical magazine. Her recovery and ability to get pregnant post-surgery was not the norm.

On top of that, Stephanie's doctors had warned her she may not be able to produce any milk for Elle. They were concerned her body may not be able to produce milk again due to any damage caused by the brain tumor. However, not only was Stephanie able to nurse Elle, she actually produced *more* milk than she had the first time with Emme. In fact, we had a freezer full of milk!

In this situation, it HAD to be God! For my wife to get through this brain surgery, with none of the post-surgery issues or side effects, conceive a baby two months later, be able to carry a healthy baby full term, *and* be able to nurse the baby for an entire year, it could *only* have been God.

I needed to remember this because I was on deck. It would soon be my turn to face Goliath.

CHAPTER 8

THE "C" WORD

(Hint: Rhymes with "Dancer")

Two Scenarios

Let's play a game of "Would You Rather." Which scenario would you rather have? (Warning: neither scenario is good.)

Would you rather:

1. Be the person with a life-threatening disease/situation?
   OR
2. Be the spouse of the person with a life-threatening disease/situation?

Think about this for a second. Which of these two scenarios would you rather have?

Unfortunately, my wife and I have experienced both.

In scenario #1, you might die. In scenario #2, you might see the person you love the most in this world die. Which is worse?

I have actually had this conversation with Stephanie in the past. Without hesitation, we both had the same response.

We would rather be scenario #1 *every* time.

Cramp in My Jaw

Now it was my turn to take on Goliath. This battle started for me as we were preparing to go to the so-called "Happiest Place On Earth"— Walt Disney World. At that time, Emme was four years old and Elle was five months old.

Over the past few months, I had started to feel something similar to a cramp in my jaw after each time I would yawn. As I would try to rub out the cramp, I noticed my jaw would be twitching for a little while afterward. I didn't think too much of it. However, in the area where I would get these cramps, something was starting to grow.

While packing for our vacation, I remember making a comment about my jaw to Stephanie. Apparently, I asked her if I should be concerned about this thing on my jaw. I turned my head to show her what I was talking about and she was immediately concerned.

Actually, the look on her face was probably closer to scared than concerned. Stephanie made me promise to go see our doctor as soon as we got back to Columbus. Although I did not want to, I agreed.

I Do Not Like Going to the Doctor

As soon as we got back from "The Most *Expensive* Place On Earth," Stephanie called our family doctor and made an appointment for me. Not only did she book the appointment, but she also asked her parents to watch the girls so she could go with me. This would be the first of countless appointments Stephanie would be going to with me.

As we waited in one of the rooms to be seen, I could tell my wife was nervous. I didn't know what was growing on my jaw, but I didn't think it was going to be anything serious. When our primary care physician came in, I explained how I noticed something on my jaw and how my wife was forcing me to get it checked out. Then I turned my head to the right to show her the now golf ball-sized growth on my jaw and the doctor's facial expression went from nice and calm to "What the @&?# is THAT?!"

She became wide-eyed and said, "THAT doesn't look good!"

No crap, Dr. Sherlock!

Despite the ~~unprofessional~~ reaction (in my opinion), she was helpful with referring me to a specialist at The James Cancer Hospital.

I *Really* Do Not Like Going to the Hospital

The following week, I went to the hospital for my initial consultation/appointment. My visit was with a surgeon in the Department of Otolaryngology-Head and Neck Surgery. I know…that is a mouthful. Do not even ask me how to pronounce that one big word because I have no idea. Thank God I married a nurse because I am fairly clueless when it comes to medical things. (I guess you can only be good at so many things, right?)

I learned a few things that day about myself and how NOT to interact with a surgeon. The first thing I learned was that I typically understand about fifty percent of what surgeons say. Even though I have a master's degree and consider myself an intelligent person, I *really* had to focus to follow along with whatever they were trying to explain to me. I would get lost in their medical jargon, which is why I needed my wife with me at these appointments.

The second thing I learned was it was a complete waste of time when I would ask the doctors to physically draw whatever they were attempting to communicate. Unfortunately, after I looked at the cartoon they drew for me, there was about a 0.01% chance I would be able to accurately repeat whatever they just told me. This meant, whenever I got asked a question by my wife, mother, or mother-in-law, there was not a snowball's chance I would be able to answer it accurately.

Another thing I learned was that some surgeons did not get my sense of humor. After about ten minutes of trying to explain something very complicated to me in his very thick accent, my surgeon asked if I had any questions. I responded with, "Yes. Can you please repeat whatever you just said, but this time, in English?"

I was kidding, of course. However, when I made this comment, he completely froze trying to remember if he had been speaking to me in English or not. He looked at me, very confused, probably because English was his third or fourth language. He then looked at my wife for some help. Stephanie laughed and told him not to worry about my question. She understood what he had said and would translate it for me later.

He then proceeded to ignore me for the rest of the appointment. He completely turned his body away from me and just had a conversation with Stephanie as if she were the patient. I was like the five-year-old child going to a doctor's appointment with his mom and not being allowed to talk. This was worse, though, because I wasn't allowed to color or get a sucker.

BTW, That Did Not Feel so Good

At the end of the appointment, I was told I needed to have some type of biopsy of the large mass on my jaw. They immediately got me scheduled for this procedure in another part of the hospital. As Stephanie and I waited in one of the rooms, I did not know what to expect. I soon found out that "biopsy" is a code word that means someone is about to stick a ginormous needle into your jaw. The purpose of this biopsy procedure was to take a sample from the tumor-like mass on my jaw and do a bunch of tests. The tests performed on the sample specimen would help determine what it was and then whether or not it was cancerous.

In my mind, this was not a big deal. Go ahead and put that lightsaber into my jaw and pull out whatever you want. This procedure would prove we had nothing to be concerned about, would get my concerned wife off my back, and then allow us to get on with our lives. Unfortunately, that did not happen.

BTW, that did not feel so good.

The Phone Call I Will Never Forget

Two days later, I received another of those life-changing phone calls you never forget. It was about 4:00 p.m. and I was at work when I got the call on my cell phone. I answered my phone and immediately walked away from my desk so nobody could possibly overhear my conversation. I went to a back hallway and leaned on a bookshelf to brace myself as a nurse from the hospital began to speak.

She informed me the doctors had examined the samples I had given them on Monday morning. The samples they tested came back showing lymphoma, which is a type of blood cancer. They were not sure at this point whether it was Hodgkin's lymphoma or non-Hodgkin's lymphoma. She told me I needed to have surgery as soon as possible.

Talk about a punch to the gut! That took my breath away. I was shocked. It was the complete opposite of the good news we had been praying for. This couldn't be right.

I told the nurse I didn't think she could possibly be correct. I was only thirty-seven years old. This had to be wrong. Was she sure this was my diagnosis? I remember asking her three times if she was *completely* sure the information she had just given me was correct…because I was seriously doubting it. Did my samples get mixed up with someone else's results? Did she call the wrong phone number?

Here is part of the conversation I remember having when this nurse was trying to get me scheduled for surgery:

Nurse: "Your doctor is recommending surgery for you to remove the cancerous mass on your jaw as soon as possible. We have an open slot next Wednesday morning, November 25th."

Me: "Next Wednesday? Let me check. Oh man…that is the day before Thanksgiving. Listen, we have some family coming into town from Seattle. That is actually not going to be a good time for us. What other time slots do you have available? How about sometime after Christmas? Or what about after New Year's? I really don't want this to mess up the holidays for me."

Nurse: "Mr. Mason, I do not think you understand the severity of what I am telling you. We *highly* recommend you have this surgery as soon as possible. If we could do it tomorrow, we would. However, the first time slot we have available is next Wednesday morning."

Me: "Okay. Go ahead and put me on the schedule and I will talk to my wife."

        (Stephanie gave me an earful about this later on...and rightfully so.)

As you can imagine, this was a pretty heavy moment for me. I stood in that hallway and had a really hard time trying to process what I had just heard. This could not be happening...to ME!

No freaking way!

I walked slowly back to my desk in disbelief.

Once at my desk, I just sat there and stared at my computer screen. I think I had Microsoft Outlook open at the time, but there was no way I was catching up on any emails right then. Nor was I going to be able to do anything productive either. I just sat there with a blank stare, in shock by what I had just heard. I had to get out of there.

Instead of walking down the aisle to have a conversation with my boss, I emailed him instead:

Mark, I just received a phone call from the hospital. Did not get the good report I was expecting to hear. I need to get out of here. Text me if you need anything.

Kevin

I quietly packed up my laptop and got out of there as fast as I could. When I got to my car, I didn't know where to go or where to drive. It was about 4:15 p.m. and we had a family dinner night scheduled with my in-laws at 6:00 p.m. I needed to figure out something to do because I had some time to kill. If I had more time, I probably would have gone somewhere to watch a movie. It was November, so I was not going to go to a driving range or batting cage. I am not a drinker (excluding our honeymoon), so I wasn't going to go to a bar. Instead, I just started driving.

I started driving around town…and thinking…and thinking…and praying. After about ten minutes, I had to pull over. I pulled into a strip mall off Hamilton Road, parked my car, and just broke down.

Stop Googling Your Diagnosis

After I got myself composed, I did one of the worst things I could possibly do. No, I didn't start playing real-life bumper cars in that parking lot (although a little demolition derby would have been fun).

Instead, I Googled the word "lymphoma" and start researching what it was and how to treat it. Big, BIG mistake!

As I started to research all the facts and evidence about this cancer, the devil started having a field day with my mind. Every web page I went to and every article I read seemed to have a worse outlook. Here is just one example…

> *Statistic:* One out of every three non-Hodgkin's lymphoma patients die within five years of diagnosis.[4]

Uh…*that's* not good! So, Mr. Website, are you telling me I might not live to see the age of forty?

It's kind of like the adage I heard when starting college: "Look at the person on your right. Now look at the person on your left. One of you will not be here in four years." This quote is talking about dropping out of school. That statistic is talking about death!

At that moment, a strong sense of fear came over me. What did all

---

[4] Cleveland Clinic, *Adult Non-Hodgkin's Lymphoma: Outlook / Prognosis,* September 15, 2019, https://my.clevelandclinic.org/health/diseases/15662-adult-non-hodgkins-lymphoma/outlook–prognosis (accessed September 27, 2019).

of this mean? How did I get this? How was I going to tell my wife? How was I going to hide this from my family at dinner?

Just like I did years earlier, I reached out to my close friend, Micah. I tried calling, but it went straight to voicemail. He responded with a text stating he was at a conference in Seattle.

Micah: "Is this important?"

Me: "Yeah, bro, this is important. I REALLY need to talk to someone."

He texted back that he would call as soon as he could get out of whatever meeting he was in. About an hour later, Micah called while I was at my in-laws' house for dinner. I politely excused myself from the table and walked outside to the driveway. Again, I did not want anyone to overhear my conversation.

I then spilled my guts to Micah and told him the news I had received. What should I do?

At that moment of time, Micah was a calming influence and an absolute godsend for me. He essentially told me to "stop Googling your diagnosis!" He then told me to stay calm and focus on the next step. Wait until the girls went to bed that evening and then have a serious conversation with Stephanie. He then prayed with me and said to keep him updated with things. What a great friend. Thank you again, Micah. You were an absolute gift to me in that critical moment of my life.

Tough Conversation

Later that night, after we put the girls to bed, I had the tough conversation with Steph. As we sat in bed, I told her about the phone call I had received earlier in the day and the crushing news they had delivered. She assumed I didn't have good news to share after seeing me excuse myself from dinner earlier that evening. However, she handled it like a champ (par for the course). We decided we would have Thanksgiving by ourselves that year and fight this battle together. That night, we also agreed we were going to trust God no matter what.

A Wife's Perspective
(Written by Stephanie Mason)

I knew it! As soon as he turned his head, I knew exactly what I was looking at. My nursing brain had a good idea of what our future could look like.

This is the time when I feel I should be open and vulnerable with you. If I am going to be totally honest with you, I was really mad at Kevin. We had just had our second miracle child, survived my electrocution, then the brain tumor, and now my husband had something growing on his jaw. To make matters worse, he did not think it was a big deal! Men, if you have an abnormal growth somewhere, go get it checked. It's abnormal because it does not belong there!

But one thing I have learned from Pastor Gary is to NOT speak death or curses over someone with our words. I looked at Kevin and told him he needed to IMMEDIATELY call and get an appointment with our family doctor. He said he would, but I think I ended up scheduling it because he tends to put things off when it comes to doctor appointments. The next day, we left for Walt Disney World with our five-month old and four-year-old. For months, I honestly thought he was just gaining weight. He had stopped going to the gym as consistently as he once did and was sleeping a lot more than usual. As we stood in line with our two little girls to see the Disney princesses, all I could see was the mass protruding from his jaw. I tried to savor every second of that trip because I could feel the battle that would be waiting for us when we got home.

Roles Reversed

Next step.

That was the *only* thing we were going to focus on—the next step.

Wow. What a wife. In sickness and in health. For better or worse. We were in this together. In a weird way, our roles were now reversed. Stephanie was the spouse on the sidelines. I was the one facing Goliath.

Challenge accepted.

Can you see it? There was an "abnormal growth" on my jaw.

CHAPTER 9

SURGERY...THEN WHAT?

Next Step: Game Plan

Even though we had been through some crazy stuff before, I knew this battle was not going to be easy. The ride we were about to go on might turn out to be downright scary at some point.

Before soldiers go into a battle, they have to prepare. They don't just show up all willy-nilly, hoping for the best. If you have ever read or watched anything about special forces, like the Navy SEALs, you will find out they are the most prepared, most rehearsed, most ready for battle. They have a game plan.

That was what Stephanie and I did. We had to prepare for battle. We decided to come up with a game plan in regards to how we were going to battle this cancer diagnosis. Our initial game plan was:

- ❖ Do not Google or independently research anything related to cancer.
- ❖ Limit the people we would share this news with.
- ❖ Study what the Bible says about healing.
- ❖ ONLY focus on the next step.
- ❖ Trust God...no matter what.

We would add to this list as time went on.

We agreed to NOT get on the Internet and research anything about lymphoma, treatments, outcomes, and so on. This was going to be tough for me because I like to research everything. But now was not the time. Not in this situation. I knew staying away from all the articles, statistics, facts, and so on would be best for me. Not researching this would help us focus on God, keep us in faith, and keep us from potentially freaking out.

This reminds me of the story about Peter walking on the water with Jesus (Matthew 14:25–33). In the middle of a storm, Peter got out of the boat and walked on the water toward Jesus. When Peter was focused on Jesus, the storm had no impact on him. However, when he looked at his surroundings and noticed the storm he was in the middle of, then fear and doubt crept in. As soon as he took his eyes off Jesus, Peter began to sink until Jesus reached out His hand to save him.

My storm was called cancer. I would be fine in the middle of my storm as long as I kept my eyes on Jesus.

We also agreed to only tell a handful of people. We were not going to blast this news from the rooftops. We would *only* tell immediate family and our closest friends. There would be absolutely *zero* Facebook or social media posts about my health.

Here are my reasons why I didn't want anything posted on social media:

1. At this critical stage, I was not going to allow any Facebook friends or acquaintances to write my obituary. No, thank you! I am a firm believer in the scripture *"death and life are in the power of the tongue"* (Proverbs 18:21). I realize people mean well and have good intentions. However, I was not going to let nonbelievers or immature Christians speak death over me.

2. I didn't want the attention and I didn't want anyone's sympathy. What I wanted was like-minded believers who were going to stand in faith with me and believe God for my healing.

3. I didn't want anyone to think my wife might be single in a few months. Nope! Not happening!

Steph laughs and rolls her eyes every time I mention #3, but I have a good idea what might happen. I might have family members ~~ON MY SIDE OF THE FAMILY~~ start the application process for Stephanie to become the next "bachelorette." I am kidding…but not really.

I realize my wife would say "no" to even the suggestion of her going on a TV dating show or the thought of going on some type of a date without me. However, I also know if I weren't around and Channing Tatum showed up, my wife might say, "I guess I could do lunch. I mean, a woman's gotta eat!"

Next Step: Talk to Pastor Gary

Part of our game plan was to tell immediate family members and close friends the news before I had surgery in less than one week. I will spare you the details from those meetings, but they went as you might expect. Everyone was so incredibly encouraging and definitely made me feel loved.

It was very touching to hear people tell me how much they loved me and what I meant to them. The compliments and heartfelt messages I received were kind of like what people might say about me at a funeral. This was, obviously, much better since I actually got to hear them…and wasn't lying in a casket.

However, I do want to share with you the conversation we had with our pastor from Faith Life Church. I cannot begin to tell you how much I admire and respect Pastor Gary Keesee.

After the 9:00 a.m. service that Sunday morning, Pastor Gary and his wife, Drenda, stepped off the stage and stood near the front of the church. Stephanie and I approached Pastor Gary and asked if we could speak with him for a minute. He obliged and I then gave him a brief summary of what was going on. I told him I had been diagnosed with cancer, was scheduled to have surgery in a few days, and was confused with how this could be happening. We felt like we had been in faith and was not expecting a terrible report like this. I thought God healed people. Why am I still being instructed to have surgery? Shouldn't sickness and disease just disappear?

Typically, when you tell someone you have been diagnosed with cancer, they will make a sad face, OR might have a gloomy disposition, OR maybe act a little bit surprised, OR possibly tell you "I am so sorry." A normal person might even tear up a little bit after hearing your news. Not Pastor Gary. Here is proof that he does not fall under the "normal person" category. When I told him I had been diagnosed with cancer, his response was…no response.

The man didn't even blink at my life-threatening news.

I was confused by his non-reaction. It was as if I had just told him something about the weather. I thought maybe he didn't hear me, so I decided to repeat the "C" word a second time to ensure he heard me. But this time, I would make sure to clearly enunciate my words. If he wasn't hearing my words, then hopefully, he could read my lips.

So I repeated the message to him again. "I had been DIE-AG-NOSED with KAN-SIR!"

Pastor just looked at me, waiting for me to finish talking.

"THAT'S NOT GOOOOOD!"

Then I realized he had heard me the first time. Pastor Gary was not giving me an "I don't care about what you just told me" type of non-reaction. Instead, he was giving me an "I am not fazed by what you just told me" type of a non-reaction. Time and time again, he has witnessed God come through for him, his family, and many others. He was not going to freak out about some bad news I heard from a doctor.

The instructions he then gave me, I believe, helped save my life. He didn't tell me he was sorry to hear my unfortunate news. He didn't tell me sometimes the Lord giveth and the Lord taketh away. He didn't even let me cry on his shoulder! Nope. None of that. It was not time for a pity party. It was time for me to gear up mentally and spiritually for the battle I was about to face.

Pastor Gary stepped closer to me, put his hand on my shoulder, and looked me straight in the eyes. Here is what I remember him telling me:

(This is from my and Stephanie's memory. It is not verbatim since I did not record our conversation.)

Pastor: "Kevin, right now I believe you need to prepare your-self for a battle in your mind. Satan is going to want to bring fear against you. You need to be strong. Get in the Word. Protect your mind. Watch your words. Speak life! Do NOT let anything negative creep in. Jesus took those stripes on his back for your healing. I believe you are healed. It just has not manifested yet. Being in faith doesn't mean you ignore what a doctor tells you. However, if you do need to have surgery, that doesn't mean you did something wrong or that you were not in faith. Of course, we have seen at times where God has instantaneously healed someone. Other times, we need to be in faith for our healing and trust God to direct our path. This could even mean aligning you to the right doctor to treat a cer-tain disease. Stay in faith and keep trusting God. He will give you the grace to walk this out."

Next Step: Meet Jud

Pastor Gary then prayed for me and Stephanie. After he finished praying, he asked if I had ever met Jud (I had not). Jud had battled leu-kemia a couple of years earlier and our pastor wanted me to meet him. So he immediately said let's go find him. I followed Pastor Gary as he started walking around the church and we eventually found Jud. Pastor explained how I had been diagnosed with cancer and wanted him to share his own cancer story with me.

Then Jud took out his phone and started scrolling through some pictures. After finding the picture he was looking for, he turned his phone around to show me.

Let's just say I was…shocked. OMG!

The picture was a selfie of him. His neck was swollen with what appeared to be large tumors everywhere. His neck looked like my jaw multiplied by fifty. I was thinking, *Jud, you win!* Whatever story he was about to tell me was *definitely* going to be worse than what I was going through. He then proceeded to tell me this picture was of him two years earlier when he was at The James Cancer Hospital (same place I would be having surgery). I am guessing Jud is probably only three to four years older than me, so he would have been going through cancer treatments in his mid-to-late thirties like I was. Doctors told him the cancer was so widespread throughout his body they only gave him about four days to live. How about THAT for some bad news! I am guessing hearing that might have ruined his day. I wonder if Jud drove around the city crying like I did. Probably not.

Hearing this gave me a little perspective…and hope. It reminded me there is always someone out there who is going through something much worse than me. It also gave me hope because Jud was standing in front of me, looking strong and healthy, after literally being given *days* to live. I, obviously, wanted to hear more of his story. He gave me his business card and told me to contact him anytime. He said he would love to tell me more over coffee. I definitely was going to take him up on his offer. However, I needed to get through surgery first.

Next Step: Surgery

What a turn of events. Last Wednesday morning, the only concern I had was hitting all the deadlines at work. The next Wednesday morning, I was having surgery to remove cancerous lymph nodes from my jaw. What a difference one week, or even one moment, can make.

The only surgery I had previously had was getting my tonsils out when I was in first grade. Not exactly major surgery.

While On the Subject: According to my mother, I used to tell people that I could remember being born. The folklore goes that I told some family and church members that I saw bright lights and windows everywhere when I was born. When my mom overheard me telling someone this, she quickly informed me there were no bright lights OR windows in her labor and delivery room. After thinking about it for a minute, my mom realized I was confusing my experience of waking up from anesthesia when I had my tonsils removed with when I was born. I only had one surgery in my life, but it was apparently pretty traumatic for me!

I just texted my mom to confirm how old I was when I was telling people this. Her response: thirteen years old. SERIOUSLY?! Wow...I was a stupid kid.

Thirty years later, my second surgery was going to be a little more serious. I remember getting wheeled into the surgery room, it being freezing cold, and only seeing eyes. No faces. Thankfully, all the people in masks seemed to have pleasant demeanors, which helped ease my nervousness. Someone told me to start counting to ten as they put the anesthesia mask over my mouth. I think I made it to five before I was out. As soon as I was asleep, it felt like I woke up, and surgery was over. That was a crazy quick nap!

Thankfully, my throat felt better than I expected it to after waking up. (Also, I wasn't confused with thinking I had just been born.)

However, I was in no mood to eat or talk. Steph came into whatever room I was in and was sooooooooo happy to see me. She filled me in on the details regarding what the doctor had told her. Surgery was successful as they removed two lymph nodes from my jaw that were almost an inch and a half in length.

Now I just wanted to get home.

Best Nurses Ever

When I got home, I had the two best nurses in the world taking care of me. I had my wife helping me with whatever I needed. I also had Emme, who is a miniature version of my wife, acting like some kind of emotional support nurse for me. My four-year-old nurse would crawl into my bed and give me hugs and kisses to help with the recovery process. Then she would cuddle beside me until I fell asleep. Moments like these just make me melt inside. I love being a dad.

> ***While On the Subject:*** When Stephanie was pregnant with Emme, we prayed our unborn child would get the absolute best qualities from each of us. I briefly mentioned this to one of my close buddies, Nick, who then informed me this meant I was "actually praying to God that my child would look nothing like me." I laughed because I thought he was kidding. After Emme was born, I soon realized that Nick was not kidding. Emme was the spitting image of my wife. Soooooo…I guess you could say our prayers were answered.

Next Step: Best Coffee Meeting *Ever*

The week after I went back to work, I had an early morning meeting scheduled with Jud. We met for coffee at a nearby Panera Bread. At this point:

- ❖ It was two weeks after my surgery to remove the cancerous lymph nodes from my jaw.
- ❖ I was officially diagnosed with non-Hodgkin's lymphoma.
- ❖ My next doctor's appointment was the following Thursday.
- ❖ I was told to expect to start sixteen weeks of chemotherapy at that appointment.

Jud was another godsend for me. He did not know me at all but was so incredibly kind and generous to spend an hour of his time to meet. After getting some coffee, I sat down with him and briefly explained what was going on. I then shut up and started taking notes.

Jud, in his words, told me his cancer *victory* story, along with everything he and his family had gone through. I know we're not handing out any trophies here, but if we were, Jud's story would win every time. Hearing him talk about his experience really helped encourage me and strengthen my faith, especially at a time when I needed to hear some encouragement. He also gave me some homework to do, such as buying a special water device and reading a few books he recommended. Whatever he was telling me to do, I was going to do it.

Then Jud completely surprised me when he posed this question:

Jud: "Kevin, do you know *why* you have cancer?"

Me: "I have no idea. My doctors don't even know. They think it could be hereditary. Stephanie has told me *numerous* times she thinks it could be from the energy drinks I've drank over the past couple of years. Thankfully, I had a few doctors shoot down that theory in front of my wife. One of my doctors even admitted to drinking some himself! The other day, I started thinking maybe it could be from our cell phones?"

Jud: "No, no, no. None of that. Kevin, you need to know this cancer is a spiritual attack against you!"

Me: "What? Why?"

Jud: "Satan is afraid of the man you *might* become! He is trying to take you out because he's afraid of the impact you *might* have for God someday."

Wow. That gave me goose bumps.

Next Step: Homework

I immediately started on the homework Jud gave me and added these items to our game plan:

1. Bought a FireAngel Ozone water purifier — I started drinking this filtered water every day with organic lemon juice squeezed into it for some taste. (This was one of the recommendations from Jud.)

2. Researched healing scriptures and printed about thirty of them onto 4×6 pictures and posted throughout our house. — I wanted to see the Word everywhere I went as a reminder that Jesus died for my sins AND my healing. There were healing scriptures on every mirror, every door, and every appliance in our home.

3. Watched my words — Stephanie and I both agreed to speak life over our health and our lives. We were going to do our absolute best to not say anything negative. I was surprised at how hard this was at first because I would catch myself saying something negative at least once a day. I wasn't aware of this bad habit, but it got easier and easier after making a conscious decision to change. I was determined to be the most positive person at work and everywhere I went.

4. Became a bookworm — Here was my reading list:
   - ❖ *365 Days of Healing* by Mark Brazee
   - ❖ *Healed of Cancer* by Dodie Osteen
   - ❖ *Hung by the Tongue* by Francis P. Martin
   - ❖ *Know Your Enemy* by Norvel Hayes
   - ❖ *Kingdom Thoughts* by Gary Keesee

This homework helped prepare me physically, spiritually, and mentally for battle.

Next Step: Appointment with Dr. Blum

The next step eventually became the appointment of all appointments. I was scheduled to meet with Dr. Blum from the Oncology Department at The James Cancer Hospital. She would be in charge of my cancer treatment process. I was a little nervous about this appointment but was absolutely believing for a miracle. I was expecting the doctor to look at me and say I could go home because they had removed all the cancer cells during surgery. That did not happen.

At this appointment, Dr. Blum informed me there were over thirty different types of non-Hodgkin's lymphoma. My particular type was B-cell follicular lymphoma. Follicular lymphoma is a slow-growing lymphoma (blood cancer) most often found in lymph nodes or bone marrow. A couple of concerns they had were:

1. This form of cancer can turn into a more aggressive type called diffuse large B-cell lymphoma.
2. The size of my lymph nodes that had been removed were fairly large. Since this was considered a slow-growing type of cancer, there could be other cancer cells throughout my bloodstream.

I then asked Dr. Blum what the odds were that the cancer cells were only in my jaw and not throughout my entire body. Her answer: less than ten percent.

It was like a scene from the movie *Dumb and Dumber*. Soooooo you're telling me there's a chance!

The doctor said it would be a miracle if this were to actually happen. Well, doctor, guess what? My wife and I serve a miracle-working God and we had already experienced *multiple* miracles. I understood what she was telling me, but I was going to continue to be in faith and believe everything was going to be fine.

Then she finally had some good news to share with us. For the time being, she did NOT want me to start any chemotherapy treatments. She wanted to see a PET-CT full-body scan and have a double bone marrow biopsy completed prior to finalizing any treatment plan for me. I didn't know what either of these were, but they sounded a heck of a lot better than chemotherapy!

Now I could enjoy Christmas of 2015…with all my hair!

Bone Marrow Biopsies Are No Joke!

By chance, do you know what a bone marrow biopsy is? Until December 30, 2015, I did not. I am glad we had committed to NOT researching things during this process. If I had Googled this procedure ahead of time, there is NO WAY I would have showed up to that appointment.

Here is the bottom half of an email I sent to family and friends that gave them a health update and my description of this procedure:

If you would like to read about my traumatic bone marrow biopsy experience, continue to read. Otherwise, you can delete this email and go on with the rest of your day.

First of all, I did not know exactly what a bone marrow biopsy was before walking into the hospital and I didn't want to know because it just sounded painful. Second of all, they gave me a nice surprise by informing me I was scheduled to have a DOUBLE biopsy that day on both hips. I have no idea how this type of pain stacks up against child birth…but I kept trying to Jedi-mind trick myself into thinking this had to be easier than anything my wife has gone through with labor. Unfortunately, this had to be the worst pain I have ever felt in my entire life. From my experience, here is what happens during a double bone marrow biopsy…

First, a nurse and nurse practitioner will ask if you have had or possibly know of anyone who has had this procedure done in the past. After you tell them no, they will then inform you (I wish I were kidding) that prior patients have stated this procedure feels like your toes are getting ripped off, and others may feel as if they are getting electrocuted, but then there are a few patients who hardly feel a thing, kind of like a bee sting. After they see your face go completely pale and you pull your hat over your eyes and then fake pass out on the bed, they will unsuccessfully try to assure you that you are probably in the minority and won't feel a thing.

They will also inform you they cannot knock you out with any anesthesia or put you to sleep with some type of choke hold to avoid the impending pain. However, the good news is they do give you a comfortable pillow to scream into and tell you there are some steel handles at the end of the bed to grab on to if needed.

After inquiring if you really, really, REALLY need to go through with this procedure, they will ask your spouse to leave the room (who, for some reason, actually wanted to stay in this torture chamber and watch). Then they ask you to lie down on the bed while they numb your back a little bit, which is pretty much the same thing as giving a pregnant woman some Flintstone vitamins to deal with the upcoming pain. Then they will ask you to not move at all while they insert a needle the size of a turkey baster into the top of your hip. Then you realize the pain you are feeling while they are sawing a piece of bone off your hip is because THEY CANNOT FREAKING GIVE YOU ANYTHING EXCEPT A PILLOW!

They also forget to inform you that guys in their thirties have much denser bones than their typical patients in their sixties and seventies, which tends to make it more challenging to cut through. Don't worry, they will remember to give you this little detail AFTERWARD.

Next, they allow you to scream into that pillow for the following ten to fifteen minutes and white knuckle the courtesy bed handles while periodically reminding you to breathe in through your nose and exhale out through your mouth. They will then randomly tell you, "You are doing so good!" as if you are a two-year-old sitting still in the barber chair for your first big boy haircut. After they finally get the bone specimen out of the left side of your hip, they will ask you with a completely straight face if that hurt or not. Not only are these two people TERRIBLE at measuring the pain tolerance of this procedure, but they should have been able to tell from the fifteen minutes of my loud, painful screams that this was no tickle fight. They will then con-gratulate you because you are now halfway done with the procedure and will start on your other hip whenever you are ready. THAT, my friends, is what a double bone marrow biopsy is. You are welcome.

Kevin

A Wife's Perspective
(Written by Stephanie Mason)

When the nurse practitioner was ready to start Kevin's double bone marrow biopsy, I remember being asked to leave the room. I was actually hoping they would allow me to stay so I could watch, but unfortunately, they would not allow me to. I gave Kevin a kiss on his cheek and told him he would do great. "You got this, babe!"

As I sat in the lounge, I remember praying, checking my phone, and then praying some more. Finally, one of the nurses came out to get me. She told me they were done with the procedure and that my husband did amazing. I was very anxious to get back to Kevin and see how he was doing. When I entered the room and saw my husband…let's just say he did not look like what I was expecting. He was pale as a ghost, leaning back in the chair, with his hat pulled down over his eyes.

He looked like he was in a lot of pain, so I was afraid to even touch him. Instead, I walked over to his side and asked if he was okay. He pulled his hat up and had a glare on his face that said, "Does it look like I'm okay?"

Next Step: January 7, 2016

This was the day we went back to see Dr. Blum to discuss the results of the body scan, biopsy, and my treatment options. At this appointment, she informed us that all my tests came back showing the cancer had NOT spread throughout my body.

Yeah, that's right! SO YOU'RE TELLING ME THERE'S A CHANCE!

Yeah, baby! That "less than ten percent chance" just turned into one hundred percent!

This was literally another miracle we experienced and had been believing God for. The doctors reiterated to me how rare this was.

Thank you, Jesus, for my healing!

They also reiterated to me that I was not out of the weeds yet. They still needed to zap whatever remaining cancer cells were around my neck and throat area with radiation. I was ready for the next step, especially since that step did NOT involve any chemotherapy.

However, I soon found out that radiation is like an evil cousin of chemotherapy. Those treatments can result in your wife having to take you to the emergency room.

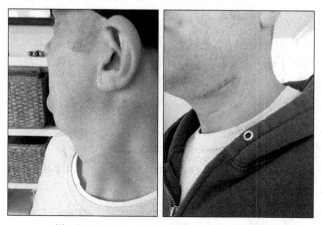

The BEFORE and AFTER surgery pictures.
It looks like I was in a knife fight... and lost!

I learned that cuddling with your daughters really helps with the recovery process.

CHAPTER 10

FROM RADIATION TO RINGING THAT BELL

Another Health Update (Email to Friends)

Below is an excerpt from the final email I sent to family, friends, and coworkers in January 2016. I will show you the bottom half of the email where I shared a couple of funny stories from my visit to the cancer hospital.

Let me start this by stating how incredible my wife is. Not only is she an amazing wife and mother, but is also an experienced registered nurse. Stephanie has been especially helpful during this process, since most of the time, I am not even sure what the doctors are telling me. My wife is able to decode all the medical jargon for me.

However, if there is one superpower that my wife has, it is that she has an absolutely incredible pain tolerance. This is a woman who was electrocuted in 2007, had brain surgery in 2014, delivered two beautiful babies, and disgustingly wakes up every morning at 5:00 a.m. excited for life and ready for her kettlebell workout. On the flip side…if there is one sizeable flaw in my wife, it is that she does not understand, cannot comprehend, or, to be more blunt, does not sympathize with people who may not have this same superpower (i.e., her husband).

Example #1

One of our very first visits to The James went something like this...

Resident Doctor:	"Mr. Mason, I need you to stick out your tongue for me please."
Me:	"Uh-oh, I don't like this little exercise."
Wife:	"You'll be fine."
Me:	(Stick out my tongue halfway.)
Resident Doctor:	"I need you to stick it out a little further please."
Me:	"AAAAHHHHHH... @$$%%$#%$^%^^%$##$#%$@%!"
	(Note: This is the sound of me gagging and almost vomiting on the resident doctor's hand.)
Resident Doctor:	"Wow! That is a pretty strong gag reflex you have there! I will let Dr. Ozer try this again when he comes in."
	(Resident doctor leaves.)
Wife:	"Hey, when Dr. Ozer comes in here, why don't you PULL UP YOUR BIG BOY PANTS AND STICK OUT YOUR TONGUE!"
Me:	(Head in hands.)

Five minutes go by and Dr. Ozer comes in with the resident doctor to examine me.

Dr. Ozer:	"Mr. Mason, I need you to stick out your tongue for me please."
Wife:	(Elbows resident doctor to watch this.)
Me:	"AAAAHHHHHH... @$$%%$#%$^%^^%$##$#%$@%!"
	(Again, we have already seen this movie once before...but same story.)

Resident doctor and my wife bust out laughing together in the corner. Glad my wife was able to make a new friend so quickly. They are probably now Facebook friends.

Dr. Ozer: "Wow! That is a pretty strong gag reflex you have there, Mr. Mason."

Wife: (Still laughing in the corner of the room.) "I cannot wait to tell my parents this one!"

Wife then proceeds to tell this story about my "strong gag reflex" to her parents the next evening over dinner. Then again to my extended family on Thanksgiving. I imagine she has probably emailed Reader's Digest this story as well.

Example #2

Before starting daily radiation treatments at the cancer hospital, someone will explain to you all the potential risks and possible side effects you could experience. The laundry list of symptoms they discussed with me were both ridiculous and somewhat scary. Of course, none of these risks seemed to faze my wife.

Resident Doctor #2:   "Mr. Mason, your side effects could include difficulties with being able to swallow."

Me: "Wow…that one doesn't sound fun at all."

Wife: "You'll be fine."

Resident Doctor #2:   "There is a high probability you will experience hair loss where the four radiation beams will enter and exit your body."

Me: "Exit my body? Where is it exiting?"

Resident Doctor #2:   "The back of your head. You will probably lose hair there and not be able to hide it by wearing a hat."

Me: "Oh crap! I know this will sound kind of stupid, but I actually just kind of grew my hair out. How long will this last?"

Resident Doctor #2:	*"Not too long. Probably about six months."*
Me:	*"SIX MONTHS!"*
Wife:	*"Really? You'll be fine. We can Google you a new hairstyle."*
Resident Doctor #2:	*"You may also experience loss of your taste buds."*
Me:	*"That sounds terrible. How long could that last…not very long…like maybe six months?"*
	(Note: That was sarcasm to the doctor, which she did not catch.)
Resident Doctor #2:	*"No, that one could be permanent."*
Me:	*"WHAT?! It sounded like you just said 'PERMANENT'!"*
Resident Doctor #2:	*"I did…but that one is only in extreme cases."*
Wife:	*"Kev, you shouldn't have to worry about that one. You are getting a lower dose of radiation. You'll be fine."*
Resident Doctor #2:	*"Mr. Mason, there is also a very small percentage of patients who will turn into leprechauns."*
Me:	*(Head in hands.)*
Wife:	*"You'll be fine."*
	(Full disclaimer: I actually made up that last one. I stopped listening after hearing symptom #72, so it is more probable than not it was actually on her list of 847 possible side effects. However, I did have my head in my hands most of the time…and kept hearing my wife telling me, "You'll be fine.")
Resident Doctor #2:	*"Okay. Any questions?"*
Wife:	*"Yes. Are there any risks with potentially getting pregnant during his radiation treatments?"*
Resident Doctor #2:	*"Let me check."*
	(Silence)
	(Silence)
	(Silence)

Resident Doctor #2:   *"No risks. It is fine if you were to get pregnant during his treatments."*

Wife: *"Oh good. You made me nervous there for a second."*

(After hearing this comment, here was my reaction inside my head...but was smart enough to not say it out loud.)

Me: *"REALLY! NOW YOU ARE NERVOUS?! Glad to know the possibility of me turning into the Lucky Charms guy didn't bother you! We are DEFINITELY going to talk about this when we get in the car!"*

Folks, I love you. Please keep me in prayer this week.

Kevin

Perspective
(Written by Stephanie Mason)

I feel the need to clarify what you just read. I am a nurse who empathizes with people all day every day. HOWEVER, I will laugh every time my husband gags on a tongue depressor when it barely touches his tongue. Also, when I was telling Kevin he would be "fine" during that conversation about possible side effects, I meant it as, "Babe you got this! You'll be fine." Apparently, that somehow got lost in translation with him.

Next Step: Radiation

My cancer treatments started on January 26, 2016. The plan was to go through thirteen treatments across a three-week period. My treatments were scheduled at 8:00 a.m. each morning before heading to work.

Like prior appointments, I was only focused on the next step. I did not know ahead of time what radiation treatments were or what they might entail. I would find out whenever I got there.

Here is the first question I was asked after walking into the radiation room:

Nurse: "Mr. Mason, are you claustrophobic by chance?"

Me: "No. Uh…why do you ask?"

Nurse: (In a very sweet, no-big-deal-kind of a voice.) "With this procedure, we have to make a cast-like mold that will go from the top of your head down to the middle of your chest. The mold will cover your face, which tends to freak out some patients. If you are a little claustrophobic, we can typically give you some type of a sedative."

Me: "Uh…no thanks. You don't need to get the tranquilizer gun out for me today."

It soon became very apparent why some patients tend to "freak out" on them. They had me lay on a cold table with my shirt off while three people hovered around me and then put a warm, mesh-like blanket over my head. For a split second, I thought I might have accidentally signed up to get waterboarded.

They told me to "not move *at all*." That sounds like an easy enough request, until they put this mesh like blanket over your head, face, and shoulders and start poking larger holes around your eyes, nose, and mouth so you can see and breathe easier. After fitting you for this cast, the nurses will then "lock" you to the table with the cast they just made. It's kind of like a straitjacket, but for your face. This thing is super tight and makes it impossible to move your head. You would have to be David Blaine or Criss Angel to get out of this contraption.

The whole process took about twenty minutes. Not fun, but I'll choose this procedure resembling a waterboarding over chemotherapy any day of the week. Afterward, one of the nurses explained why they have to make this cast and freaking lock me to the table. With radiation treatments, they are zapping a very specific area of my throat with radiation beams to kill any remaining cancer cells. If I were to accidentally move during one of these treatments, the beam of radiation could zap me somewhere else and do permanent damage. If I were to sneeze, cough, fall asleep, or accidentally jerk after dreaming about falling off a cliff (speaking from experience), the radiation beams could hit something that I do not want to have zapped.

After she explained it to me like that, I was completely cool with getting locked to the table.

Does Your Pizza Taste Like Cardboard?

After the first couple of treatments, I started to feel the effects. I woke up on the third day exhausted and decided to sleep in. I made the executive decision to skip my scheduled treatment, sleep in, and then go to work. I thought the treatments were like work where, if you feel terrible, you are allowed to call off and then come in the next day. I soon found out that medical folks tend to blow a gasket when their patients do not show up for their regularly scheduled cancer treatment. Unfortunately, missing appointments is HEAVILY frowned upon at cancer hospitals. I got a nice phone call from a hospital nurse asking if I was okay, you know, since I had not shown up that day. I told her I was feeling really tired and would "catch the next one." That answer did not fly with her and I was promptly informed this was NOT how cancer treatments work.

Apparently, if you have thirteen radiation treatments scheduled IN A ROW, you are supposed to actually show up to those thirteen appointments IN A ROW. I was not allowed to pick and choose when to show up, like I did with classes in college. I had to attend these treatments EXACTLY when they were scheduled. The effects of these cancer treatments would diminish if patients (i.e., me) did not follow their protocol.

Roger that!

However, after my eighth treatment, the side effects really started to kick in. In an attempt to help me feel better, my wife decided to go get my favorite pizza, which is a locally owned place called Eagle's Pizza in New Albany, Ohio. We would always share a large, extra cheese pizza on top of my pint salad with blue cheese dressing. Due to my diminishing appetite, Stephanie only ordered pizza this time.

Unfortunately, when I took that first bite, my favorite pizza tasted like cardboard. I was shocked. I took a second bite…and again, it tasted like cardboard (or what I think cardboard might taste like). I asked Stephanie if her pizza tasted okay, and she said it tasted amazing (like it normally does). After eating one small square of my cardboard-tasting pizza, I couldn't eat anymore. Dinner was over for me.

The next morning, I went downstairs to eat some Honey Nut Cheerios with a cut-up banana. When I took a bite, it tasted like I was eating cereal in spoiled milk. I smelled the milk and it smelled fine. It was nowhere near the expiration date listed on the gallon. Then I took the milk upstairs for Stephanie to smell. She smelled it and then taste-tested it for me. The milk was fine. Then it hit me. My taste buds had changed!

The Wrath of My Mother-in-Law

Sadly, I was now having to deal with a major side effect (and it wouldn't be the last). The doctors had said I "might lose" my taste buds, which didn't sound like that big of a deal to me. I told Stephanie if broccoli and kale were going to taste the same as pizza and ice cream, then I was going to load up on leafy greens and get super healthy. However, I may have misinterpreted what "lose your taste buds" meant. To me, *losing* your taste buds meant you can't taste *anything* because you *lost* them. This seemed simple enough to me. I didn't think I needed my wife to translate this for me. However, my taste buds completely changed! That is different…and in my opinion, MUCH, MUCH WORSE! Now everything tasted terrible, including water. This was NOT good.

After I threw my perfectly good breakfast in the trash, I went upstairs to shower. It's hard to explain, but I was feeling a little off that morning in addition to my taste buds. While in the shower, I remember getting really dizzy, blacking out, and then falling down on the shower floor. I am not sure how long I was keeled over on the floor, but I eventually regained my balance and finished my shower. I thought this was just another side effect hitting me and part of this crazy process. I was so distraught that morning with all these new physical symptoms that I didn't even mention to Stephanie what had happened in the shower before getting in the car and driving. DUMB!

Thank God, I made it to the hospital that morning for my next treatment. What if I had another dizzy spell while driving ~~75 mph~~ on the freeway?

When I got to my appointment, one of the nurses asked me if I was okay.

Nurse: "How are you feeling after the weekend?"

Me: "I'm fine."

Nurse: "Are you sure? You don't seem like yourself this morning."

Me: "I'm just getting really annoyed right now."

Nurse: "Why?"

Me: "Because I started getting some side effects this weekend that I honestly was not expecting."

Nurse: "What kind of side effects?"

Me: "Just dumb stuff…like my taste buds changing on me. I really don't want to talk about it because whatever I say is bothering me will result in someone prescribing another pill to take. I don't want any more pills. I get it…this is part of the process. I'll be a big boy here and not complain. I'm ready to just move onto my next treatment."

We proceeded to complete radiation treatment #9 and not once did I tell anyone about my dizzy spell in the shower. As soon as I left the hospital, I called Stephanie. While driving, I told her I was starting to feel kind of sick and was going to pull into a parking lot somewhere to take a quick nap. I thought it would be a better idea to fall asleep in a Target parking lot instead of my work parking lot. If a coworker were to see me sleeping in my car, they might think I was being lazy or something worse. The last thing I wanted was to get woken up from a nap by someone pounding on my window to ensure I wasn't dead.

Steph told me NOT to pull over because she would not know where I would be if something were to happen to me. Smart woman. She mentioned going to her parents' house to take a quick nap, which was not too far away from work. She would call her mom to let her know I was going to stop by.

When I walked through the door at my in-laws' house, Brenda looked at me and said something like, "Whoa! You don't look so good." I mentioned I was not feeling well and then something about keeling over in the shower earlier. She asked if I had told this to Stephanie or anyone at the hospital. I told her no because I thought this was part of the process. I then witnessed the wrath of my mother-in-law, which, up until that point, I had successfully stayed away from. She started yelling at me. I mean, *really yelling* at me!

"HOW COULD YOU NOT TELL ANYONE ABOUT THIS?!"

"YOU HAVE TO TELL YOUR DOCTORS WHAT IS GOING ON!"

"WE CAN'T HAVE ANYTHING HAPPEN TO YOU!"

~~"YOU ARE MY FAVORITE SON-IN-LAW!~~

~~I LIKE YOU SO MUCH BETTER THAN THAT OTHER GUY!"~~

I appreciated her concern…but she was kind of scaring me. I picked up my walking pace and quickly disappeared downstairs to their cold, dark basement. As I laid down to take a quick nap, Brenda grabbed her phone and called my favorite nurse.

We Are Going Back to the Hospital!

All of a sudden, I woke up to my wife running down the steps yelling at me to wake up.

(Why, all of a sudden, is everyone in this family yelling at me? Don't they know I'm not feeling good! Has anyone called my sister-in-law yet? Maybe she can come over here and yell at me too!)

Stephanie said, "We are going back to the hospital!"

Why? She called the hospital staff who, of course, were not aware of me blacking out in the shower and wanted to see me immediately. For obvious reasons, I was not allowed to drive myself. Brenda watched Emme and Elle while Stephanie rushed me back to the hospital.

When we got to the hospital, the nurses and doctors asked me a ton of questions. Then they wanted to run some additional tests to confirm I was not having a stroke or something even more serious. I remember the nurse practitioner coming in and telling me I needed to consider taking some time off from work to focus on getting healthy. To me, that was some crazy talk. In my mind, I was fully capable of doing both. I could continue to work a stressful corporate job, play tough guy, and get through these cancer treatments all at the same time. I only had four more treatments to go. I was almost done, right?

Then she asked me a tough question: "What is the absolute worst thing that would happen if you called your boss right now and asked to take a couple weeks off?"

This question forced me to stop and think. What is the *worst* thing that would happen?

Well, I would not expect the company to fold, our stock price to collapse, or even my department to fall apart. I guess I really wasn't *that* important. However, being in management at this company could be an absolute pressure cooker at times, especially in my department. I guess the worst thing that would happen was my team struggle to get everything done in a timely manner without me. It would force others to pick up more responsibilities to cover for my absence. I would also feel like I was letting people down. It was already a tough department to work in. If I were not there, it would make things even more challenging for the people I worked with. I would hate to make my coworkers do more or have to stay longer hours because of me.

Whoever this woman was, she was pretty darn good. I am guessing this was not her first rodeo in regards to dealing with stubborn folks. After finally agreeing to her request to temporarily step away from work, she told me she would give me some privacy so I could call my boss.

Wait…what?

You want me to call my boss…like right now?

Yup.

I then realized she had been playing nice with me during this entire conversation. If I didn't call my boss right then, she was probably going to call my employer for me. ~~I was now surrounded by a bunch of women who cared about me…and wouldn't listen to me!~~

Reluctantly, I took my phone out and called my boss to tell him I had some bad news to share. Thankfully, he was incredibly supportive and told me to take as much time off as I needed. He mentioned he was actually relieved to hear this was the bad news I was calling him about. He was concerned I was calling to tell him something much worse.

Next Step: Focus on Getting Better

I am proud to say that I went to work every day after surgery and through the first two weeks of my cancer treatments. However, that was as far as I could go. I have no shame in admitting I had to tap out.

The longest amount of time I had ever taken off work was two weeks for our wedding, honeymoon, and to move into our new house together. However, that was over a decade ago when I was younger in my career with minimum responsibilities. Now, I was going to be off work indefinitely, but it was definitely NOT going to be a vacation.

As my final week of treatments progressed, the side effects continued to get worse and worse. By the end of the week, everything I put in my mouth tasted terrible. Nothing tasted normal or was even remotely appealing to me anymore. Most food also smelled disgusting. My nose was like Stephanie's when she was pregnant. I had to hold my nose each time I attempted to eat something. I also had to hold my nose when going to the grocery store. I tried walking into Kroger's one morning to pick up a prescription and almost passed out from the smell. The overwhelming smell of food and spices in the grocery store punched me right in the face. Then at home, whenever I would open the refrigerator door, the smell again would be overwhelming.

During one of those rough days, my mom's husband, Art, was so kind in trying to help. He went to the store and bought me about eight different flavors of Gatorade, Powerade, and Vitamin Water. I think the lemon lime Gatorade was the only flavor that tasted okay to me. Thankfully, I was able to drink this…a little bit at a time.

Ring That Bell

By the time I got to my final appointment at The James Cancer Hospital, I could barely talk. I could only whisper when trying to speak because my throat was a mess, internally, from the radiation. Stephanie decided to attend my last appointment with me to see what it was like, plus celebrate my final cancer treatment. At the conclusion of that treatment, a nurse mentioned there would be a little ceremony out in the waiting room for me, which I was completely unaware of. So we walked back to the waiting room area, and one of my nurses went up front to get everyone's attention. In the room were all the other cancer patients, their family members, their friends, and some other hospital staff. She announced, "This is Kevin Mason and he just finished his final cancer treatment!" She read a short poem and at the end of it told me to ring the bell hanging on the wall three times.

While On the Subject: I had seen this bell every day in the waiting room but didn't know what it was for. Like a little kid, who can't keep his hands to himself, I almost rang it during one of those days to hear what it sounded like. I am sooooo glad I didn't do that. I had no idea this bell was actually for a special ceremony with cancer patients. Remember...I was not Googling or researching anything. I was only focused on the next step.

My next step was to ring that bell three times.

I rang the bell and I will never...ever...ever...never forget that moment. As soon as I finished ringing the bell, everyone in the room stood up and applauded me. Think about that for a second. There were people in this room who were *terminal* cancer patients. People who did not have a lot of hope of living much longer. These people, with their friends and family, were now applauding *me!* Even if my throat had not been fried by that point, I would not have been able to speak. Just an unbelievable moment.

I can remember two significant moments in my life, where I have felt completely overwhelmed with emotion at the drop of a hat. The first was on my wedding day when the church doors opened and I saw my beautiful bride in her wedding gown.

The second was when I rang that bell. Talk about a *heavy* moment.

My fellow cancer patients then started coming over to congratulate me and wish me luck with my recovery. I mean...I could only nod my head at them, point to my heart, and mouth the words "thank you." I hope they could read my lips because no sound was coming out of my mouth.

I very rarely tell this story to anyone because I cannot tell it without crying. Now I know I can't type it either without crying!

Unfortunately, this would not be my last time at the hospital. Unbeknownst to me, in just a few short days, I would be back for a ~~fun~~ ten-day sleepover.

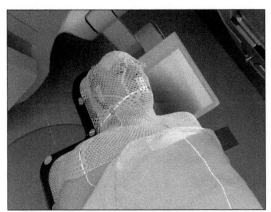

Here is a picture of me being 'locked' to the table during my radiation treatments. The mask made some weird looking indentations all over my head and face. I was constantly trying to rub them off during my drive to work. I didn't want to scare anyone.

This was the morning of my final cancer treatment... and when I got to ring that bell.

CHAPTER 11

KEVIN'S HEALING

My Road to Recovery

After I finished that final treatment at The James, my health started to get worse. Actually, much worse.

As soon as we got home, I was exhausted and just wanted to go to bed. Unfortunately, I was having a tough time with swallowing. I started to panic at first but then remembered this was one of the major side effects they had previously warned me about. I then learned the hard way that it's difficult to do a few important things when you can't swallow... like sleep...or eat...or drink...or talk. This was incredibly frustrating and hard to live with.

The next morning, Stephanie started to get concerned about me potentially becoming dehydrated. Being the awesome nurse she is, she drove me to her work and gave me an IV to get some fluids in me. Sadly, this turned out to be like putting a Band-Aid on a shark bite. I was going to need a lot more than that one IV.

By evening, I was *really* struggling. I told Stephanie, if I didn't start to feel better by the next day, I would probably need her to take me somewhere. Guess what?

I didn't get any better. I only got worse. As I mentioned earlier, this was the most miserable, physically, that I had ever felt. I was exhausted but struggled to sleep more than two hours at a time. I was hungry but couldn't eat much. When I would try to drink something, I would immediately start hacking and coughing. Every time I took a drink, it felt like the fluid was going down the wrong pipe (because it was). I finally had to wave the white flag. I needed medical attention. My tough-it-out attitude had to end because I was in too much discomfort. I couldn't live like this any longer. Stephanie called my mom and her husband, Art, to come watch the girls and then rushed me to the emergency room.

Next Step: Back to the Hospital

I knew I was probably in bad shape by the time I finally decided I needed some help. However, I soon found out I was in worse shape than I thought. When Stephanie dropped me off at the hospital entrance, I didn't have the energy to walk from the front door to the check-in desk across the emergency room floor. (Why did they put the desk so far away from the front door?)

When the hospital staff saw me *slowly* walking like an eighty-year-old, a nurse brought me a wheelchair and immediately took me back to some side room to check me in. I must have looked pretty bad since they didn't make me sit out in the waiting room for about five hours like you normally do at the ER.

After taking my vitals, performing some tests, and meeting with a doctor, they informed me I was severely dehydrated and had pneumonia and a 104-degree temperature. They wanted me to spend the night to keep an eye on me.

While trying to sleep that night, I attempted to take a small drink of water and immediately threw it up. I was coughing and hacking and couldn't get it under control…all from one little drink of water. I was then informed that I no longer was allowed to eat or drink *anything*. The only thing I was allowed to swallow was my own saliva. If I needed a drink, I was to swish and spit it out in a tray.

The next morning, the doctor decided they needed to send me back to The James Cancer Hospital. I was pretty happy to hear this because I had the utmost confidence The James would know what to do. I was then given my first (and only) ride in an ambulance. Unfortunately, this excursion was as a patient instead of a healthy person wanting to go for a joy ride.

BTW...have you ever ridden in the back of an ambulance? It was NOT what I expected. I thought it would be the smoothest ride ever, but it turned out to be the most uncomfortable ride ever. That is really bad considering I was lying on a bed the entire time!

For some reason, I also expected the ambulance to turn on the siren, put the pedal to the metal, and start dodging traffic every which way to get me to The James. Isn't that what they do when they transport important people to the hospital? Or does that only happen on TV? I assumed they would do that for me, but I obviously assumed wrong. They *might* have only gotten that beast up to 55 mph on the freeway. There were probably school buses passing us on my trip to the hospital. If I had the ability to talk, I would have yelled "GO FASTER!" like my four-year-old does when I give her piggyback rides. I wasn't expecting this trip to feel like I was on *The Dukes of Hazzard*, but geez, at least make the ride a little exciting for me!

Next Step: Ten-Day Sleepover at the Hospital

After getting to The James, they ran their own set of tests on me and decided I needed to be admitted. Yay! I get to extend my sleepover at another hospital (that was sarcasm). They hooked me up to multiple IVs and reiterated I was not allowed to eat or drink *anything*. They would hydrate me through my IVs and give me some medicine to help alleviate any hunger pains until they could figure things out.

I do not know how my wife did it. Stephanie was an absolute rock star. She was helping take care of me at home, then visiting me in the hospital, working part-time, nursing an eight-month-old (who decided this would be the best time to start teething), AND took care of our four-year-old. She must have not slept much during those six months.

By day three of my sleepover, I was still only able to whisper when trying to speak. However, I began writing on a whiteboard and doing some sign language to communicate with folks. When I tell you that I started doing some "sign language," what I really mean is I started playing charades to communicate. I have no idea how to do sign language, but I acted out whatever needed to get my message across. For example, I would put my hands together beside my head to indicate I was tired, or I would hold my arm out in front of me and act like I was trying to press a button when I needed the remote control. You know…the important stuff.

Along with not being able to talk, I still couldn't sleep much because of my swallowing issue. Thankfully, they were able to give me some melatonin to help with getting to sleep. They also had a specialist come to my room and figure out a way for me to drink something again without gagging. I was told my throat was pretty much fried internally from the radiation treatments. Whenever I tried to drink something, it was going down my windpipe instead of my esophagus. This led to me getting fluid in my lungs, which then led to me getting pneumonia.

At the end of the session with the specialist, we discovered whenever I would take a drink of water and then tilt my head toward my right shoulder, the fluid would go down the correct pipe. That meant, over the next two to three weeks, any time I would eat or drink, I had to tilt my head to the right side and then try to swallow. Annoying as it was, I was thrilled to be able to drink something again.

The next thing I had to deal with was the awful taste of everything I put in my mouth. On top of that, my heightened sense of smell made a lot of the food have a foul stench to them. The hospital food they would bring me smelled absolutely disgusting. I remember trying to eat a couple bites of the hospital meatloaf and it being just unbearable. I would try to hold my nose, chew, tilt my head to the right, and then swallow after each bite. Not fun.

Also, my schnoz was ridiculously sensitive. So much in fact that I began smelling a distinct body odor from each person who came into my hospital room. I had one particular male nurse trying to help me who almost made me pass out each time he got near me. I was doing my best to hold my breath but could not do that for very long when he started asking me questions. I thought it would be rude if he saw me with my cheeks all puffed out, holding my breath while trying to have a conversation with him. Instead, I asked Stephanie to request a new nurse because his BO was too offensive for me. (I would have put this request in myself but wasn't exactly sure how to do my "sign language" for that.)

Overall, I was in the hospital for ten days and nine nights, but it felt like *weeks*. I started to get really uncomfortable sitting in that hospital bed all day every day. I forced myself to walk around the floor two to three times a day for fifteen minutes. I was told to either get out of bed and walk or get a feeding tube. Easy choice. Whenever I had visitors, I would ask them to take a walk with me.

After day seven of my pajama party, I soooo needed to get some fresh air. I initially wanted to open a window, but quickly found out you can't open hospital windows (makes sense). So I asked if there was anywhere I could go to get some fresh air (like a local bowling alley). Thankfully, they told me I could go down a few floors to an outdoor patio for some fresh air. I probably looked pretty weird walking through the little food court on the fourteenth floor while pushing my IV coat rack alongside me. I didn't care, though, because I was desperate to get some fresh air. As soon as I opened the patio door, I quickly remembered it was February and only about twenty degrees outside. Again, I didn't care. I was happy to get some fresh air for two minutes at a time…because I only had my hospital gown on.

Next Step: Beg Doctor to Let Me Go Home

By day nine, I really wanted to get out of the hospital. Not only did I have cabin fever, but I was *really* missing my family. Stephanie did her best to visit most days, and we allowed Emme to visit one time, which we later regretted.

Looking back, I wish we would not have allowed Emme to see me in that condition. Although I loved seeing my four-year-old at the hospital, it scared her to see her daddy in such bad shape. She saw me pretty sick that day, and for months afterward, would not let go of me each night when I put her to bed. Emme would not stop hugging my neck because she was scared that whenever she woke up, I might be in the hospital again. That broke my heart. Lesson learned.

To get out of the hospital, I was going to have to show some signs of improving. My doctors were primarily concerned about two things, the first being my temperature. It took over a week to get my temperature back down to under 100 degrees. My temperature came down once they had gotten the pneumonia taken care of. This coincided with me being able to speak closer to normal again, which was helpful. No more having to play charades with visitors. But they were really concerned about my struggle with eating and drinking. While in the hospital, they had been hydrating me constantly through multiple IVs. If I were at home, there would be no IVs to hydrate me. They did not want me to go home for a day or two, struggle to eat, and then see me back at the hospital in worse shape.

Thankfully, on day ten my doctors finally signed off on allowing me to be discharged. However, their approval came with a very clear warning before I left the hospital. If I did not eat and drink sufficiently when I got home, they would have to give me a feeding tube.

Like everything else related to cancer, I didn't know exactly what getting a feeding tube might entail, but it did not sound good. Months later, I looked it up on WebMD, which confirmed it is NOT good.

Living With a Feed Tube

❖ *"You might have a critical illness like cancer and lack the strength to eat enough to stay healthy. If you're unable to eat and drink like you used to, a feeding tube can help you get the nutrition you need and lower your chances of choking. Depending on your situation, the tube will run either through your nose or into your stomach or intestines."*

❖ *"A feeding tube can be uncomfortable and even painful sometimes. You'll need to adjust your sleeping position and make extra time to clean and maintain your tube and to handle any complications. Still, you can do most things as you always have. You can go out to restaurants with friends, have sex, and exercise."*[5]

Wow…good to know a feeding tube could allow me to *"do most things as I always have."* Thank you, WebMD! My life would not be worth living if I couldn't go out to restaurants, exercise, or have sex with friends. (Wait…did I misread that?)

OMG…This Is Tough

I was now going to have to eat to live. My new full-time job was to eat and drink as much as possible. I started by living off vanilla Ensure drinks, which I actually thought were only for senior citizens. Thank God for those Ensure drinks because they got me through the initial days when I was struggling to eat. Outside of this liquid diet, I would do my best to eat *something* each day. I desperately needed protein. As I mentioned earlier, food still smelled and tasted horrible. I literally had to give

---

[5] WebMD, *Living With a Feeding Tube,* n.d., https://www.webmd.com/digestive-disorders/living-with-feeding-tube#1 (accessed September 26, 2019).

myself a pep talk every time I tried to eat. "Come on, Kevin! You can do this! Be a big boy and eat your vegetables!" I would hold my nose and do my best to not worry about the taste. Each time I ate, it probably looked like I was competing on the show *Fear Factor*.

Then I had *another* wrench of a side effect thrown at me. My new symptom was dry mouth, which meant very little to no production of saliva. Another thing I didn't know about radiation treatments is they can damage your salivary glands. Once my body stopped producing saliva, it made it *very* difficult to chew and swallow food. Having no saliva in my mouth meant it could take me up to an hour to eat a small cup of yogurt. An hour! For comparison, I guess it would be kind of like trying to brush your teeth with a bunch of toothpaste in your mouth but no water. The yogurt would just swish around and around in my mouth because I didn't have any saliva.

It also meant, if I were to try to eat anything of substance like a small piece of a chicken nugget, I would have to chew and chew and chew and chew to get it down.

After two days at home, it hit me, "OMG…this is tough!" Just to get through one day was tough. Tough to sleep. Tough to eat. Tough to drink. On top of that, I would have to hold my breath or hold my nose every time I opened the refrigerator door so the smell wouldn't blast me in the face.

One more thing I realized is that I was losing a lot of weight. And losing it quickly. I lost twenty pounds in less than three weeks and thirty-seven pounds in total. I had not really noticed the massive weight loss until one day when I was walking down the steps to get an Ensure drink and my sweatpants fell down to my ankles. I almost tripped on my pants while going down the steps. Thankfully, I was quick enough to grab hold of the railing before tumbling down the stairs.

While On the Subject: When we went to church that Easter Sunday, I had to dress in something other than sweatpants. When I put my watch on while getting ready, it immediately slid down my arm. I didn't know I had chunky wrists before these cancer treatments. Apparently, I lost some girth around my waist *and* wrists! I actually had to take my watch to a jeweler to get a link taken out. Just another funny thing I did not expect to happen.

My Breaking Point

By the morning of day three at home, I was struggling mentally. Even with all my praying, believing, staying positive, and being in faith, I had a breaking point. This day would be my low point and I had a mental meltdown.

After Stephanie left for work, I received a phone call from my radiation oncologist following up with how things were going. I told her terrible. I was still struggling to eat and basically surviving off my Ensure drinks. I was starting to feel really weak again, probably from not eating as much as I needed to since returning home. She told me all of this was normal. She said it typically takes patients six months or longer to start feeling healthy again with getting their taste buds and saliva back.

SIX MONTHS?! OR LONGER?!

Please tell me you are joking, doc! That was the absolute *worst* thing someone could have told me right then.

I immediately called Stephanie who was at work. I asked her how long it took her uncle to get his taste buds back after he went through cancer treatments. She had been keeping this information from me because she did not want to potentially discourage me. But I was now asking her point-blank.

Her answer: six months.

At that moment, I broke.

Me: "Steph, I can't do this! Six months? SIX MONTHS! Do you know how hard it is for me just to get through one day?! Go ahead and just drive me back to the hospital…because I can't do this for six months. No way! Six months sounds like a decade to me right now. If this lasts six months, I am going to lose my job. My career could be over. Gosh, being off work this long…we could lose our house! Everything we have worked for could be gone…just like that! I am in shock right now. I can't believe this. SIX MONTHS!"

Steph: "I know, honey. We are going to pray your taste buds and everything else will be restored…quickly."

When Kevin Called
(Written by Stephanie Mason)

I cannot even begin to describe the feeling of helplessness I experienced during the several months of Kevin's surgery, radiation treatments, hospital stay, and then recovery at home. I was trying to be so positive and encouraging to my husband, but I was exhausted. I was trying to go on appointments with Kevin, plus work, and take care of our toddler and baby.

When he called, I was doing my best to be encouraging over the phone. But honestly, folks, I was beginning to lose my battle as well with staying positive. I remember being at work and the tears started to flow. Thank God for my coworkers that day. I had not cried from the time he had gotten his cancer diagnosis until now. But I was now feeling scared that I would have to take my husband back to the hospital to get a feeding tube. I was scared I was going to mentally lose it and not be the pillar of strength that Kevin and my girls needed me to be. I was tired, I was scared, and like my husband, I was feeling defeated.

Next Step: Speak the Word

After having a rough day mentally and physically, I was again having a rough night with trying to sleep. I laid there, thinking about the discouraging prognosis I had received earlier that day. It was near midnight when I decided to walk downstairs to get some water. Then for some reason, the picture I had taped on the pantry door caught my attention. It was a photo with the scripture Romans 8:11 (NIV): *"He who raised Christ from the dead will also give life to your mortal bodies because of His Spirit who lives in you."* I quietly read this scripture out loud. As soon as I finished speaking the scripture, there was like a jolt of energy that went through my body.

Then I walked over to the fridge and read out loud the scripture posted on that appliance. Psalm 118:17 (NIV): *"I will not die but live, and will proclaim what the Lord has done."* Same thing. When I spoke the Word, another jolt of energy went through my body.

I wanted to keep going. So I walked over to our kitchen cabinets and read the scripture posted there, and then to another scripture. It felt like, at that moment, I was starting to receive my physical healing. My physical, mortal body was gaining strength!

I was so excited, I wanted to test something to see if anything had changed. I knew I felt something. This couldn't just be all in my head. How could I test this moment to prove my body was starting to heal? How about opening the refrigerator door and sticking my head in it? Great idea. That was exactly what I did. I opened the door, stuck my head in, and took a big whiff. Guess what? This time, I didn't get punched in the face with a terrible smell.

Okay...let me try that again. I backed away from the fridge for a moment and then shoved my head back in to take another whiff. Same result. My sense of smell was completely normal!

I immediately went back to bed and woke Stephanie up. I told her what had just happened in the kitchen. I believed my body was starting to heal when I physically *spoke* the Word. I was so excited and gave my wife a big hug. Stephanie whispered she was happy too and then rolled over and went back to sleep.

I guess I got her at a bad time.

> **Lesson learned**: Do NOT wake up a sleeping momma who is still nursing your baby…even if you have life-changing news to share with her. There is a good chance she will be awake in about two hours with a hungry baby. Just wait to give her your news then.

Next Step: My Healing Process Continues

The next day, my healing continued to manifest. That day, I was able to eat some yogurt and it taste normal! Then the following day, for some reason, I asked Stephanie if she could get me some Skyline Chili to taste-test. I had only eaten this maybe one or two times previously, but I remembered that Skyline Chili was really thin compared to others. This time, my experience was the same as the last. It tasted like chili!

I still couldn't taste many things…but that was okay. I was now able to eat *something* that tasted normal again. The next day, I was able to eat another item, and the day after that, something else. My saliva also started to regenerate, which was amazing. I could now begin to eat some solid food, get more protein in my body, stop the massive weight loss, and most importantly, NOT have to get a feeding tube. Each day became a baby step toward my full recovery. Each day, I became noticeably better.

Best. Phone. Call. Ever!

About six weeks after I had finished my radiation treatments, I got THE phone call of my life. March 24, 2016 is a date I will remember forever.

On this day, one my doctors from The James Cancer Hospital called to inform me she had reviewed my most recent tests and body scans. In her opinion, I was now "cancer free." BEST. PHONE. CALL. EVER!

This was actually the same doctor who had called me weeks earlier and told me it would be *months* before my taste buds came back. Now she was calling to tell me I was cancer free.

Wow…another AMAZING moment for me. Cancer cells were gone from my body! God is so good! After getting off the phone and taking a few breaths to process what just happened, I called my rock star. Stephanie was at work when I called her. After sharing the news with her, the phone went silent.

Then I heard the tears of joy. My Goliath had been defeated.

We had won the battle *and* the war.

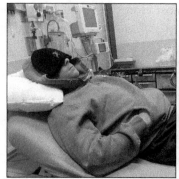
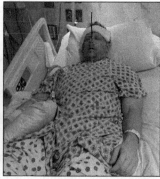

I was in pretty bad shape when I was admitted to the hospital. Stephanie, thank you for taking such flattering pictures of me. You could have at least told me to say, "CHEESE!".

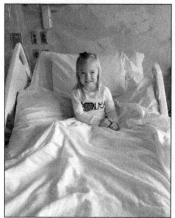
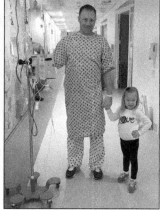

We allowed Emme to come visit her daddy one time at the hospital. I think she got more attention from the nurses that day than I did.

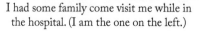

I had some family come visit me while in the hospital. (I am the one on the left.)

No, this is NOT a picture of me trying to rob a bank. However, this is what I looked like each time I had to go out in public.

CHAPTER 12

A Few Other Funny Moments

A Couple of Funny Moments

I asked my mother to read a small section of this book prior to submitting to the publisher. Her response was not exactly two thumbs up because, in her words, she did not like me "making fun of cancer." I realize I do not share the same sense of humor or personality as my mother. However, I pray the feedback I received from my mom will not be the same response or experience for you. I understand people can view things from a very different prism than mine, so I want to be crystal clear with folks that I am not "making fun of cancer." Trust me when I say I realize cancer is no joke. I have lived it!

With that disclaimer out of the way, I want to share a handful of moments that were funny. At least they were funny to me! Thankfully, the cancer treatments did not steal my sense of humor. Hope you enjoy a few of these stories.

Mom, you should go ahead and skip to the next chapter. You will probably not like this one.

Post-surgery Reaction

When I went back to work after my surgery to remove the cancerous lymph nodes, I had a two-inch long incision on my left jaw. I was not allowed to cover it with a bandage or anything, as it needed the airflow to heal properly (see picture at the end of chapter 9). To say I was a little self-conscious that morning on my way to work would be an understatement.

As I had expected, within the first few minutes at my desk, I got the type of reaction I had been nervous about. In an attempt to be funny, here is what one of my direct reports told me:

Joe: "Kevin, I am glad you told us in our meeting last week you were having surgery."

Me: "Why is that?"

Joe: "Otherwise, I would have thought you tried to kill yourself over the weekend."

However, his comment made me almost fall out of my chair in laughter. After seeing my reaction, the rest of my team then realized it was okay for them to laugh as well. Joe had comically addressed the "elephant in the room" and his comment actually helped calm me down and relax.

Joe, thank you for making me laugh that morning. That was a good one! However, I would not recommend you say something like that to anyone else at work...unless you like getting phone calls from HR.

What Facial Hair?

Once I took a leave of absence from work, I pretty much stopped shaving. Shaving was the least of my concerns. Since I wasn't going to work every day, I decided I didn't need to look like a professional every day. My full-time job was to get healthy, which in my mind did not include shaving. By the time I was admitted to the hospital, I had a good week-long stubble on my face.

By day two of my hospital slumber party, I needed to figure out how to take a shower. I had IVs in both arms, attached to something that looked like a coat rack, with a box that made a lot of loud beeping sounds. How the heck was I supposed to get all of these IV cords untangled and get into the shower with this coat rack?

After my favorite nurse (Stephanie) helped untangle the IV lines and unplug the cord to my coat rack, I very slowly took a shower. After getting out of the nice warm shower, I dried my face off with a towel. When I removed the towel from my face, it looked like there was hair all over my towel. I immediately looked in the mirror and all the hair from the entire left side of my face was gone. Half of that week-long beard was now in my towel!

One side of my face was as smooth as a baby's and the other side was as masculine as a lumberjack. Not really...but I'll keep telling myself that. What was no joke was that I looked terrible. Stephanie was shocked when she saw me walk out of the bathroom. She very kindly told me I needed to shave...as soon as possible. I shaved that day but did not shave again until I got back home.

Then when my sister-in-law saw me a week later at our house, you would think her initial response might be, "How you are feeling, Kev?"

Nope.

Her first words were, "Cool beard, bro!"

In the grand scheme of things, losing some facial hair was not a big deal. I was blessed it was only the hair on my face instead of the hair on my head. However, I was pretty happy a few months later when my facial hair started to grow back. I was so excited, in fact, that I grew a beard. I didn't grow it just because I thought it looked good. I grew it just because I could.

My Neighbor

A few days after I got home from my ten-day pajama party, one of our next door neighbors showed up at the front door. This particular neighbor is an awesome guy and a great person to live beside. He is one of those neighbors you can text anytime to borrow a tool or ask to keep an eye on your house while on vacation. Of course, I try to do the same for him as well.

On this particular day, I apparently left the garage door up and he noticed my car was home. That prompted him to walk over to see if I could help him with something. When I opened the door, I must have looked like death (or some other really bad word I cannot think of right now).

Neighbor: "Hey Kevin, how are you? Whoa…you sick or something?"
Me: "Yeah, kind of."
Neighbor: "What do you mean by 'kind of'?"
Me: "I actually just got out of the hospital a couple of days ago and am home now trying to recover."
Neighbor: "Hospital? If you don't mind me asking, trying to recover from what?"
Me: "Cancer."

My neighbor took a step or two away from the door and almost fell off the front porch. I think he may have even grabbed onto our porch pole, which saved him from falling down a step or into the mulch bed. He said he came over to see if I could help him move some furniture, but I clearly was not in any physical condition to do that. He got out of there like a bat out of you know where!

Reactions from Work People

I ended up taking three months off work to recover all the side effects and complications I had from the cancer treatments. On my first day back to work, one of the executives at Express saw me in the hallway and tracked me down to talk.

Executive: "Hey Kevin, why haven't you been showing up to our monthly one-on-one meetings? I think you've missed the last two or three we've had on the calendar."

Me:	"Oh, I am really sorry about that. Believe it or not, this is actually my first day back at work. I had to take a leave of absence and haven't even been in the building over the last three months."
Executive:	"Leave of absence? For what?"
Me:	"Cancer."
Executive:	"Is everything okay? You good now?"
Me:	"Yes, I am feeling better now. Thanks for asking."
Executive:	"You know what you should do? You should ride in that Pelotonia race this summer for cancer research!"
Me:	"Yeah, that sounds like a great idea. Thanks."

Since this was a senior executive at the $2.2B company I worked for, I decided to smile and filter my response. However, here is what I wanted to tell him:

Me:	"Yeah, Doug, that sounds like a great idea! However, how about I try to get through one day at work here, where I don't have to take a nap in my car, BEFORE I sign up to ride in a 100-mile bike race!"

I *really* wanted to say that after his stupid suggestion that I should ride in bicycle race. Thankfully, I kept calm and decided kindness would be more professional and Christlike.

I Have to Have This Conversation AGAIN?!

When preparing to go back to work, I realized there would be a couple things I would not be able to hide. I would not be able to hide the new ~~knife wound~~ scar on my jaw or the massive weight loss. I had gone from weighing 207 pounds to 170 pounds within six weeks. I had lost so much weight my sister-in-law jokingly started calling me "High School Kevin." It was a funny nickname, but in all reality, I now weighed *less* than I did when I graduated high school.

By the time I went back to work, I had probably put a little of the weight back on, but not much of the thirty-seven pounds I had lost. Gaining most of my weight back took a few months, which led to at least one dreadful conversation each week. Every week for about two months, someone at work would randomly stop me in the hallway and ask how I lost so much weight.

One of my coworkers, Scott, happened to be with me during one of these terrible conversations. Let's just say that he was highly entertained because they would inevitably lead to some type of an awkward moment. He thought it was hilarious to watch someone's face go from "I wonder if Kevin is on that new keto diet" to "OH MY GOSH...I am so sorry I asked! I feel like such a jerk. I had no idea you had cancer!"

After experiencing one of these conversations in person, Scott was adamant I give him an update *every* time this happened to me. He said this was one of the funniest things he had ever seen at work. I guess this would be kind of funny to watch...if YOU weren't the one having these conversations *every* week!

While walking to a meeting...

Store Ops Man:	"Hey Kevin, haven't seen you in a while!"
Me:	"I know, it's been a minute."
Store Ops Man:	"You're looking lean, bro! You training for a marathon or something?"

While paying for a coffee in the cafe...

Cashier:	"I am sorry, but can I ask you a question?"
Me:	"Sure. Go ahead. "
Cashier:	"Are you in some type of Biggest Losers challenge?"

While getting coffee, I had probably the sweetest, kindest woman in the building stop me...

Store Ops Woman:	"Oh my gosh, Kevin. You look amazing! You've lost some weight, haven't you?

Me:	"Oh, thank you. Yeah, I've lost a little bit of weight."
Store Ops Woman:	"A little bit?! How much have you lost?"
Me:	"Well, I am currently down about twenty-five pounds."
Store Ops Woman:	"That is AMAZING! How did you do it? What kind of diet have you been on?"
Me:	"Uhh…you don't want to know."
Store Ops Woman:	"Yes, I do! How did you lose all that weight…and so quickly?"
Me:	"Cancer."
	(Puts hand over her mouth and is speechless. Then starts to cry.)
Me:	"No, no! I am okay. I am okay! I promise."

She had put me on the spot and I honestly did not know what to tell her besides the truth. Although I think God would have been okay if I had just lied to this sweet woman to protect her feelings. I should have made something up, like tell her I was on a cigarette diet.

Request for Cancer Research Donation

A person from another department found me while walking to the restroom and thought they might be able to get a cancer donation from me. Unfortunately for them, they did not get me at a good moment…and got my unfiltered response.

Person:	"Hey Kevin. I heard you went through a rough battle with cancer recently."
Me:	"You would be correct. That was no fun."
Person:	"Then would you be interested in donating some money to sponsor me in the Pelotonia race for cancer research?"
Me:	"No, not really."

Person: "Seriously? I thought, out of everyone here, you would be the one person most interested in donating toward cancer research."

Me: "Nope. I am actually more interested in donating money toward my own cancer bills before I start giving money to cancer research."

Person: "Oh yeah. That makes sense."

I am kicking myself now for not reversing the request back to her. I should have asked her if SHE would like to donate some money toward my "Now I Am in Debt Because of All These Cancer Bills Fund."

New IT Guy

I was in a meeting with some IT folks and there was a new guy whom I had not met yet. He introduced himself to me and then I did the same to him. He looked confused after I told him my name. He then looked at the meeting invite he was emailed, which had our ID badge pictures beside the names. My ID picture would have been taken about two years earlier. He said, "Wait…THIS is YOU?! You look nothing like this picture." The room immediately busted out in laughter. I laughed as well and said I would tell him the inside joke afterward.

Reaction from Chinese Takeout

Speaking of my ID not looking like me, I had another situation where someone questioned the picture on my ID. I was trying to pay for our Chinese takeout and gave the cashier my credit card, which had "SEE ID" in black letters on the back of the card. I typically write that on my credit cards in case they were to ever get stolen. However, only about one in fifty people actually ask for my ID (which means it doesn't work). This particular cashier was that one out of fifty who asked to see my ID. After handing him my driver's license…

Cashier:	"Sir, is this really you?"
Me:	"It is."
Cashier:	(Doing a double take.) "Dude! How long ago was this picture taken?"
Me:	"About eight months ago. I look a little different, huh?"
Cashier:	"Yeah, this looks nothing like you. Rough couple of months?"
Me:	"You could say that."

Reactions from Church People

Church people are funny. When I was healthy enough to go back to church, I was hoping to just show up in the back of the sanctuary and nobody notice. Needless to say, that didn't happen. I ended up having a lot of people come over to say hello, and got one of these three reactions each time.

Reaction #1: Person would come over to say hello but wouldn't want to get too close to me. Either they thought they might catch something if they got too close OR thought they might hurt me if they were to give me a normal hug. Instead, I would get hugs from people with only their hands touching the sides of my arms. Their body would still be two feet away from me, as if we were at a middle school dance together.

Reaction #2: Person would come over to say hello and then tilt their head to the side, give you their best scrunched up sympathy face, and say, "You doing okay?" It was the type of response you typically see at a funeral where people will tilt their head and say, "I am so sorry for your loss."

Reaction #3: Person would do a double take when they saw me, walk over, and say very loudly, "OH MY GOSH...YOU ARE SO SKINNY!"

As soon as we got in the car, I told my wife I didn't know I used to be a big, fat guy. She should have told me!

What a difference a few months can make! The picture on the left is from June 2015.
The picture on the right is from February 2016. That was a *rough* few months!

I want to give a big 'thank you' to whatever company makes Ensure drinks.
However, I never want to drink one ever again!

CHAPTER 13

From Miscarriage to Baby Joy!

Time to Try for Another Baby

As soon as my health began to feel somewhat back to normal, we wanted to start trying to expand our family again. We definitely did not feel like we were done having children yet. After going back to work, it probably took another four months for me to get my weight and strength back. At that point, it was time to try for another baby!

A Couple of Signs from Heaven

I feel like this is a good place to mention a few experiences that happened along our journey to having more children. As I mentioned before, I typically am not one of those super spiritual-type of Christians like some people are. What I mean by that is I have met people who act as if God instructs them on EVERY SINGLE DECISION they make throughout each day. You cannot have a conversation with them without hearing the phrase "God told me" *multiple* times. No disrespect here, but did God *really* tell you to eat that entire bag of Doritos?

I am a firm believer that God orders our steps and directs our paths. I also believe God speaks to people through various methods. It could be through a dream, through strong thoughts brought to your mind while praying, or through a moment of meditation. We are all different—different personalities, different communication styles, and different ways of hearing God's voice. I believe God can use different channels to speak to each of us if we are willing to listen for His voice.

I write all of that because there were two situations where we felt like we received some type of sign from heaven that we would indeed be having another child someday. For those of you who may have had an encounter with God in the past, you will understand what I am referring to. Like myself, you have seen and experienced certain things where you cannot deny that God is real. There are things that have happened that I just cannot explain. I do not have a good answer as to "how" or "why" something happened. However, I just know it absolutely, positively, and unquestionably HAD to be God. Here are two examples of that.

Example #1

When Stephanie had her brain surgery in 2014, her biggest concern was whether or not she would be able to have more children. That was her heart's desire. That desire was even greater than her own health.

While On the Subject: Mothers, from what I have seen and experienced with my wife, I cannot begin to express how much respect I have for all of you. The love you have for your children and what you do on a daily basis for your families just blows my mind. And for the women out there who may be single mothers, I cannot begin to imagine all you do and go through on a daily basis. Raising children is hard enough with two parents, let alone trying to do it on your own. As I write this, I pray you would be renewed with strength and hope and that you would feel God's love wherever you are. In Jesus name, amen.

A few days after she had brain surgery, we had a friend of ours, Tonia, come visit us at the hospital. Stephanie was still recovering and didn't want many visitors. However, she said yes to her coming to visit. When Tonia got to the hospital, she told us she had recently had a dream that felt incredibly real to her and wanted to share with us. In her dream, Tonia was at our house and saw a child. She saw the back of a child standing on some type of a bridge with blond hair and shirt off. The child's back was facing Tonia. She felt like her dream was a picture of our future child. Of course, this was encouraging news to hear because the doctors had been telling us it was extremely unlikely this could actually happen. I don't think Tonia knew this or how important it was for Stephanie (and me) to have more children.

About a year later, after Elle was born, we saw Tonia and reminded her of the dream she had shared with us at the hospital. Tonia proceeded to tell us she didn't think Elle was the baby she had seen in her dream. The child she had seen in her dream appeared to be a boy.

Say what?!

Fast forward to another year later when Tonia and her husband, Anthony, came over to our house before we all went out to dinner. I didn't realize it, but they had not been to the house we had moved to three years earlier. As we were talking, Tonia looked out the back windows of our home and saw a bridge. I had recently built a seventy-five-foot long cedar bridge that connected the deck in our backyard to the pool. As she looked out the window, she realized…THAT was the bridge! That was the bridge she had seen in her dream two years earlier.

At that moment, I think we all had goose bumps. That meant there might be another baby in our future. Wow…wow…wow.

Example #2

The second God-type moment we experienced was right around the time I was finally healthy and we had decided to start trying for another baby. Not sure if my experience has been the same as other married folks, but trying for a baby can be incredibly frustrating. Not only does it test your patience, but it can also take the fun out of the "benefits" part of being married. For the husband, it can turn the most pleasurable thing on earth into a chore-like task. Instead of enjoying a natural and spontaneous moment with your spouse, you end up hearing your wife yelling at you that we "HAVE TO DO THIS RIGHT NOW!"

It doesn't matter if you just walked in the door after a rough day at work. It doesn't matter if you just got comfortable on the couch. It doesn't matter if the only thing you want to do is relax and watch the football game. What matters is your wife getting pregnant. That means you must turn into a robot and do things on command. No pressure, right?

To be quite honest, "the pressure" was not on me. The pressure was really being felt by Stephanie. EVERY. SINGLE. DAY.

Stephanie felt pressure to get pregnant as quickly as possible due to our age and every health challenge we had faced. Then the pressure she was feeling would lead to stress. Then the stress would lead to frustration ~~with her husband~~. I know…I know! My wife's biological clock was ticking. I get it.

Having another child was *constantly* on my wife's mind. Not only was it frustrating for Stephanie to go month after month without getting pregnant, but it also became tough for her to enjoy social media. At one point, she had to take a sabbatical from it all because it seemed like all she was seeing was other women getting pregnant. She was truly happy for whoever was getting pregnant, but the comments she would read made it tough for my wife.

The comments posted would be from women who had gotten pregnant "so easy," or "were not even trying," or about a teenager getting "knocked up" and not wanting the baby, or someone else talking about their "oops baby." I can only imagine how difficult it might be to read that when you ache to have another baby.

While On the Subject: This is just my own personal opinion, but I feel like I need to mention something serious here. One of my hot buttons is when I hear someone talk about having or being an "oops baby." In my mind, THERE IS NO SUCH THING AS AN OOPS BABY!

I saw a college friend of mine moved to tears one day when he was telling me about his parents. His older brother was about ten years older than him, and he made a comment about how he had been "an accident." He said he had always been labeled as an "oops baby" and felt his parents, especially his father, had never wanted him. He felt like he had always been an inconvenience to his parents his entire life. This muscular, tough exterior of a guy teared up in front me when he told me this.

I don't know who I may be writing this for, but I want to make something very clear. Your parents may not have planned you, but God did. You may have been labeled as something other than desired or cherished, but guess what? You were wanted by God. He loves you because you are His child. You were created for a purpose. There are no accidents with God.

After one Sunday morning at church, Stephanie decided to go up front for prayer in regards to our fertility challenges. Pastor Gary's wife, Drenda, came over and prayed for Stephanie. At the end of her prayer, Pastor Drenda looked at my wife and said she really felt in her spirit that she would be pregnant by the end of the year. This was around September, so we had about three months left. This message encouraged us and reinforced our belief that God saw us in that moment. He did not forget about us. He saw our hearts' desire. To us, this moment confirmed what we had already been praying and believing God for.

The good news: we *strongly* felt Stephanie was going to be pregnant again…soon.

The bad news: I was probably not going to be watching many live football games that season.

Check It Again

We mentally held onto that prayer and continued to believe God for another miracle baby. If Sarah could conceive a child with Abraham at the age of ninety, then Stephanie could conceive a child at the young age of thirty-eight. Easy-peasy, right?

At the end of that ~~football season~~ year, we had zero signs that Stephanie might be pregnant. Regardless of how my wife was or was not feeling, we continued to *speak* and *believe* that she was going to be pregnant. Even though she had no physical signs of being pregnant on the last day of the year, my wife took a pregnancy test. The result? Negative. NOT pregnant.

What did we do? We assumed that test was a false negative...and she took another one. And guess what? That test ALSO was negative. NOT pregnant. Ugh!

My wife was starting to get emotional. Did we do something wrong? Were we not in faith? Did Pastor Drenda completely whiff when she was praying over Stephanie a few months earlier? I did my best to play male cheerleader by constantly encouraging my wife and trying to stay positive.

At moments like these, the only thing I can do is pray. I do not have all the answers, but I know God does. Regardless of the *multiple* pregnancy tests Stephanie took over those three plus months, we needed to continue to trust God for another baby.

Soooooo...you want to guess what happened next?

Like I have said previously...if I had not lived this life, I may have a hard time believing some of our stories like this one. This was pretty much straight out of a movie.

The next day, on January 1st, Stephanie looked on the bathroom counter where the two pregnancy tests from December 31st were still lying. For some reason, she had not thrown them away yet. She grabbed them to put in the trash can underneath her sink but took a glance before tossing them away. The second test kind of looked like it had a faint line on it. SO YOU'RE TELLING ME THERE'S A CHANCE!

There was actually a slim chance this over-the-counter test was showing as positive. However, she needed to confirm with something a little more "official" than this CVS pee stick. The next day at work, she took another test. The result?

Her eggo was preggo!

Uh...What Does *That* Mean?

We were excited and wanted to celebrate. Stephanie and I had been to Las Vegas twice before and had an absolute blast both times. Because of that, my wife wanted to go back to Vegas one more time to celebrate. I took care of all the travel arrangements and we planned to leave on a Friday in February. However, I got a phone call from Stephanie on Thursday before our trip, asking me if I could come home.

Come home? It was not exactly a good time for me to try to come home. I was trying to wrap things up at work before going on vacation. Why? Stephanie responded that she had gone to the bathroom and was bleeding pretty bad. Bleeding? Uh...what does *that* mean?

Dear clueless Kevin, that means she is in the process of having a miscarriage. Stop asking questions, drop whatever you are doing, and get home!

I hurried home and immediately took Stephanie to the hospital. This was not good. Not good at all.

Unfortunately, like millions of other women, this pregnancy did not go the full term. I felt terrible for my wife. This was not a situation where I was questioning God as to "why did this happen?" I was just speechless and trying to figure out what I could do to help. It was an emotional and physical roller coaster for Stephanie.

Her doctor told us it was probably not a good idea to jump on a plane and fly five hours across the country. However, she said she was *not* going to tell us we shouldn't get away for a few days. Stephanie decided she still wanted to get on that plane to Vegas. If she felt bad after the flight, we would immediately go to the nearest hospital in Las Vegas. This was completely her call.

Fortunately, we were able to go on that trip because we had an incredible time. It felt so weird with it being only the two of us. No kids. We kind of forgot what that felt like.

Thank God, I did not have to rush Stephanie to any hospital when we landed in Las Vegas. On that trip, we laughed together, we cried together, and we lost some money together. But most importantly, we started to heal together.

"You Are Not Done"
(Written by Stephanie Mason)

Leading up to delivering Elle, Kevin kept saying he wanted three kids. I would just laugh. "Sorry, babe, we are a two-kid family." Then Kevin switched his story to wanting four children, with the intent of trying to negotiate with me. His new argument was if I wanted two kids and he wanted four kids, then we should compromise and have three. (Nice try, Kevin!)

It was not that I didn't want more children. It was that my pregnancies had been really hard for me. I was sick and not just the first trimester, but the entire pregnancy. I was so nauseous and always had aversions to food and smells. My back hurt all the time and I could never get comfortable.

With that being said, I felt after delivering Elle I could finally be done with being sick and constantly in pain because I would be holding our final little girl. I guess this was true…because technically, I was holding our final little girl. But I wasn't holding a baby boy, and sometimes our plans are not necessarily God's plans. After delivering Elle and holding her in my arms, I heard God speak to me, "You are not done."

Now, ladies, you know it had to be God when you just delivered a baby and hear those words. However, I felt totally at peace at that moment. I kept telling Kevin, "I could totally do this again." I was shocked by how I felt. Total peace. Needless to say, my husband was very happy.

After we had Elle, I remember talking to Kevin about trying for another baby. I knew I heard God but also knew I was not getting any younger, so we should probably get this show on the road. But this is the time when Kevin did not have the energy he used too. Then when Elle was five months old, Kevin was diagnosed with cancer.

Skip ahead one year later, Kevin was healed and we were ready for baby #3. I don't know how to describe the feeling, but I would ache for that next baby. It was like I knew we were not a complete family yet. Someone was missing.

Years earlier, before we had Emme, I remember being at the mall with my sister after my doctors had told us to not even think about having children. I told Katie I did not care if I had stretch marks, gained a bunch of weight, or had some other physical changes to my body. I just wanted a baby. That same feeling came over me with each child before I was pregnant. I wanted our babies so bad I literally ached for them.

Some people might say, "You already have a healthy child, can't you be happy with what you have?" I can easily answer that. YES, I am so happy and feel so blessed, but I still felt like there was a void. Again, it felt like someone was missing.

The Test
(Written by Stephanie Mason)

After the miscarriage, my body needed a few months to heal. I remember talking to one of my closest friends who had experienced a few miscarriages. I knew she would be able to help me through this. During our conversation, I found out she was expecting their fourth child, and she told me she knew my time would be soon. I held onto her words of encouragement. Every day, I would remember her words and the words of Tonia and, of course, what God had spoken to me when I delivered Elle. But even after reminding myself of this each day, I still had to walk it out. I still had to battle with fear and doubt trying to creep into my mind.

The miscarriage was always a reminder of what could happen. Every day, I had to speak against negativity. We will have another baby.

At the end of June, I remember being at work, taking a pregnancy test, wrapping it in toilet paper, and putting it in my pocket. I took a few minutes in my room to pray. Then I started to gather all the supplies I would need for the day before closing the door. I took the test out of my pocket. When I unraveled it, there was one dark line…and one faint line. I was pregnant!

How Accurate Are Your Tests?
(Written by Stephanie Mason)

Of course, over the next few months, I was very sick and very tired, just like I was with the girls. This pregnancy felt exactly like the first two, so Kevin and I thought we were having another girl. I remember telling Kevin our third child will bring *joy*. Joy would be the perfect middle name for our girl. But driving home in the fall, I got a phone call from the doctor's office. Since I was older, I had to get my blood drawn for genetic testing, which would also tell us the gender of our baby. I remember answering the phone.

"Hello."

"Hello, Mrs. Mason?"

"Yes."

"Hi. I am with so and so and I have the results of your genetic screening. Is now a good time to talk?"

"HECK, YES IT IS!"

She proceeded to tell me that all the genetic screening tests came back with no abnormal findings. Then she said…

"Would you like to know the gender of your baby?"

"Yes, please!"

"You are having a boy."

At that moment my mouth dropped. "Seriously?! How accurate are your tests?"

"Ma'am, our tests are over ninety-nine percent accurate."

I started to laugh. "Then we are probably having a boy! Thank you so much."

I was shocked. A boy? But our boy's middle name could not be "Joy." But then I remembered Tonia's dream. Then I smiled and said, "It's a boy!" God always knows what is best.

Then after one of our ultrasounds, Kevin and I went to breakfast at Bob Evans. I told him how much I loved the name Ava because it had that hard "A" sound. He started to look up names. At one point he said, "What about Tate?" I loved it. Right away I thought it was perfect. But then I asked him to look up the meaning. When he looked it up, he started smiling and then chuckled.

"What does it mean?"

Kevin responded with, "It means joy."

We had our name.

The Name Game

It was around the Fourth of July when Stephanie told me she was pregnant again for the fourth (and final) time. Wow. Wow. Wow!

That was quick...and didn't require me to miss one single play of an Ohio State football game! ~~More proof that God knows the desires of our hearts.~~

I hate to admit it, but by this time, I had forgotten about the dream Tonia had shared with us a few years earlier. Stephanie and I both thought we would be having a third girl. For me, the thought of having a house full of girls would be ~~a lot of drama~~ exciting! If we were blessed with another girl, we were planning to continue the pattern we established with our first two baby names. The names Emme and Elle are considered palindromes, which are words that can be spelled the same forward *and* backward. After looking at a list of palindrome names, we were going to go with the name Ava.

But then Stephanie found out we were having a boy!

I was over the moon, thrilled at the news, but it honestly made me nervous. Boys scared me. They scared me because boys will eventually look to their dad to learn things. That meant I would have to be his hero. That meant I would have to start acting like a responsible adult!

After getting the news a little dude was on the way, we looked up a list of boy palindrome names, and immediately, our pattern came to a screeching halt.

Bob. Bub. Alla. Racecar.

Racecar? Seriously?! Why would you name your baby Racecar? Do you plan to actually like your child?

After the ultrasound appointment, we found the name Tate while having breakfast. This was perfect because we did not know anyone named Tate. What I really mean is we didn't know anyone who had ruined this name for us. Weird how that works, isn't it?

When Trying to Pick Out a Name

Let me give all the young, married folks out there a little piece of advice. When you find out you are expecting a baby, one of the fun and exciting things to do with your spouse is picking out a baby name. However, do *not* do this fun activity with anyone else in the room... because they will RUIN it for you!

I learned this lesson soon after finding out Stephanie was pregnant with our first child. We made this mistake with my in-laws who worked in the public school system for about forty years. What happens is you will say a name out loud that you like...possibly a name you may have kept a secret for a few years. Then you will watch as that baby name gets absolutely *shredded* because of someone your in-laws knew back in 1995.

I'll give you a little example of how quickly one of your names can get destroyed. I can't remember the exact name I threw out, but this is what happened:

Me:	"How about the name Sally? I kind of like that one."
Mother-in-law:	"Ugh! You can't go with Sally! Absolutely not!"
Me:	"Why not?"
Mother-in-law:	"We knew a Sally one time. Steve, what was that girl's last name, from Whatchamacallit's?"
Father-in-law:	"Uhhhhhhhhhh...gosh, you asked me too quick... uhhhhhhhhhh. Gosh, you know...I can't remember."
Me:	"Listen, I don't care about her last name. But why didn't you like Sally?"
Mother-in-law:	"She was a floozy!"

As you can see, when you have in-laws who have known a lot of people, it can be a little challenging to come up with a name that hasn't already been ruined for them.

(This might explain why the name "Kevin Jr." was instantly vetoed.)

Tate Keller Mason

Thankfully, the name Tate was unique...and perfect for us. This name was also unanimously endorsed by relatives...quite possibly because they didn't hear it prior to him being born.

Then on February 24, 2018, we got to meet our "Baby Joy." Baby Tate turned out to be a biggin'! A healthy nine-pound, five-ounce baby boy. Tate Keller Mason was born just over one year from the day Stephanie had the miscarriage. What an answer to prayer. Another miracle baby.

Remember that dream Tonia had? It *definitely* came true.

After having Tate, our family felt complete.

CHAPTER 14

WHAT DOES ALL
THIS MEAN?

The Final Chapter

Gosh, life can be hard. Sometimes life can be *really* hard. Over the past fifteen years, Stephanie and I have privately cried a lot of tears.

Unfortunately, there are many other people in this world who have also cried a lot of tears. Just like when Stephanie was electrocuted, you cannot look at the exterior of a person and understand what they might be going through. You cannot begin to understand the challenges or personal Goliaths someone is facing by just looking at them.

As I write this, the scripture Romans 8:28 (NIV) is what keeps coming to my mind. It reads, *"And we know that **in all things** God works for the good of those who love him, who have been called according to his purpose."*

This scripture really hits home with us. Sometimes, bad things happen to good people. I believe we live in an evil world where Satan will do anything and everything he can to destroy you (John 10:10). However, Stephanie and I have seen God turn every terrible incident that has happened to us over the past fifteen years into something good.

It's truly amazing what God has done for us. Healing. Health. Children. Family.

Looking at our family picture, I feel so incredibly blessed. Recently, one of the new hires at work was telling me about her family and then asked if I had any children. I then showed her the picture you see at the end of chapter 13. Her response was, "Wow. It looks like you hired an actress and some child models to sit with you for a picture. It's just too perfect!"

That may have been the funniest backhanded compliment I have ever been given. If she only knew the amount of faith required for all of us to even be sitting in that picture. Quite honestly, without faith… there would be nobody to take a picture of. None of us would even be here today.

Without faith, Stephanie could have died back in 2007. I could have died in 2016. These three children would have never been conceived. I remember one of Steph's doctors reviewing her medical history and just shaking her head. She said, "You guys have been through a lot! This is not normal."

Then after Stephanie's electrocution, doctors told us they didn't have much medical research to reference with her type of injury. It was because the other people had died.

These last fifteen years have not always been fun. They certainly have not been easy. However, we can stand here today and tell you unequivocally that God is good *in all things*.

What Did I Learn from This?

Why did Stephanie get electrocuted? Why did she develop a brain tumor? Why did she have a miscarriage? Why did I get cancer? Why did we struggle time and time again to conceive a baby?

I don't know. How is that for an enlightening answer?

However, here is what I do know…

- ❖ I know that God helped us fight every Goliath that came our way.
- ❖ I know that we learned to trust God in every battle we faced. Those battles could not be fought with our own strength. We

had to put our faith in God and believe His word to be true. We had to trust God to fight these battles for us and He did.

❖ I know that doctors have good intentions and do their very best to help, but they are not the final say. God is. Our help comes from the Lord.

❖ I know that our words are absolutely critical. Death and life are in the power of the tongue. What you say, what you speak, and what you pray can absolutely move mountains.

What Will *You* Do?

I believe there will come a point in each of our lives where we just have to trust God. We like to be in control. We like to think we can figure things out on our own. If you can figure it out on your own, then you don't need to look to God for help. God wants us to trust Him with our lives…not just when we can't figure it out. Why do we look to God as our last resort when we are in a mess or when nothing makes sense? We should be running to Him as our first step, not our final step…*after* we have exhausted all other resources.

Let me ask you some tough questions:

– What will you do when things don't make sense?
– What will you do when faced with a crisis?
– How will you win the battle in your mind against fear?
– How are you going to handle hearing bad news?
– Are you going to try to run to your parents? Or are you going to put on the whole armor of God and prepare for battle?

Trust me, there is no helicopter or snow-plowing parent who will be able to face this for you. You will have to rely on God to help you fight your own battles.

Throughout every health crisis and Goliath we faced, I had zero control over the situation. My education couldn't help me. My friends and network of contacts couldn't help me. My level of intelligence and experience couldn't help me. Money couldn't help me. Only God could help me.

I want to encourage you. You may be facing a hopeless situation like we have. Whatever you are facing, God can help you too. He is no respecter of persons. If He will do it for us, He will do it for you. Our God is good *all* the time. He is our savior. He is our healer. In Him, I will put my trust.

What a Difference a Year Can Make

The church we attend in Ohio has an annual tradition called "What a Difference a Year Can Make." This might be my favorite thing our church does. Each year, the media team will interview a few families in our church and video-record their personal testimonies. The incredible stories and testimonies shared are about what God has done in their lives over the past year.

We have seen personal testimonies shared by folks in our church who have been healed of leukemia (my friend, Jud), or a man healed of PTSD from his time in the military, or from parents whose baby was pronounced dead at birth. That baby woke up thirty minutes later at the hospital and is now a completely healthy girl in our church. We have seen and heard miracle after miracle of God's healing power.

Three years ago, I sat in our church and watched that year's version of "What a Difference a Year Can Make." I was merely days away from starting my cancer treatments and had been preparing for my battle. I watched as a man named Aaron talked about how Jesus healed "all." I looked it up and there are *numerous* scriptures that talk about how Jesus healed "all" or "everyone" (Matthew 8:16, Matthew 12:15, Luke 6:19, Luke 4:40, Mark 6:56).

Guess what? I am an "all"! Aaron is an "all." YOU are an "all"!

I was so encouraged by all of these stories. Like Revelation 12:11 (NKJV): *"And they overcame him by the blood of the Lamb and by the word of their testimony."* This was exactly what I needed to hear. These stories of hope helped strengthened my faith. I knew I was going to be fine. One way or another, cancer was going to have to leave my body.

At that moment, I looked at Stephanie and pointed toward the screen. "THAT will be us someday. Someday, we will have a story to share. Our story is not going to end here. This is just a chapter. Our story is going to have an amazing ending."

Just as we *spoke* and *believed*, our story ends with us living a life of healing and hope. This has been our journey.

About the Authors

KEVIN MASON has served in various finance and accounting roles during his 18-year career with Fortune 500 companies and Big Four public accounting. Kevin graduated from Ohio Northern University with an Accounting degree and received his MBA from Ohio University. He is also a Certified Public Accountant and financial consultant to Storyside Church in Bellville, Ohio.

STEPHANIE MASON graduated from Capital University and is a Registered Nurse. Stephanie has worked in a cardiac step down unit, labor & delivery, and surgery. She currently works at a medical spa and lives in Columbus, Ohio, with Kevin and their three children.

Find out more about Kevin and Stephanie at www.kevinandsteph.com.

CPSIA information can be obtained
at www.ICGtesting.com
Printed in the USA
LVHW022050051121
702523LV00003B/14

9 780578 681658